0-8057-6645-6   **$21.95**

T · H · E
ROMANCE
OF THE
R · O · S · E

The thirteenth-century allegorical poem *The Romance of the Rose* was the most widely read secular text of the Middle Ages and the most influential work of medieval French literature. Begun in the early 1200s by Guillaume de Lorris, the *Rose* was originally shaped as an allegorical love poem intended for an aristocratic audience. Several decades later, the poem was extended by Jean de Meun, whose work broadened the poem's appeal to include academics and the middle classes. No longer simply a poem written in the tradition of courtly love literature, the *Rose* became a radical questioning of life, embracing complex issues such as the relationship between men and women and the role of religious orders in society. It also presented a timeless, philosophical rumination on the relationship between faith and reason. Read by Dante and Chaucer, among other leading European literary figures, the *Rose* laid the foundation for the development of a secular literature for the middle classes.

Heather Arden provides readers of this challenging work with a detailed outline and plot synopses invaluable to understanding the poem and the history of its creation. Arden's discussion of the cultural traditions to which the two

The author at work. From E Museo 65, fol. 66.

Reproduced with the permission of the Bodleian Library, Oxford University.

The Romance of the Rose

By Heather M. Arden

University of Cincinnati

Twayne Publishers
A Division of G.K. Hall & Co. • *Boston*

The Romance of the Rose
Heather M. Arden

Copyright 1987 by G.K. Hall & Co.
All rights reserved.
Published by Twayne Publishers
A Division of G. K. Hall & Co.
70 Lincoln Street
Boston, Massachusetts 02111

Copyediting supervised by Lewis DeSimone
Book production by Janet Zietowski
Book design by Barbara Anderson

Typeset in 11 pt. Garamond
by Compset, Inc., Beverly, Massachusetts

Library of Congress Cataloging in Publication Data

Arden, Heather, 1943–
    The romance of the Rose.

    (Twayne's world authors series ; TWAS 791. French
literature)
    Bibliography: p.
    Includes index.
    1. Guillaume, de Lorris, fl. 1230. Roman de la Rose.
2. Jean, de Meun, c. 1305?—Criticism and interpretation.
I. Title.   II. Series: Twayne's world authors series ;
TWAS 791.   III. Series: Twayne's world authors series.
French literature.
PQ1528.A89   1986   841'.1   87-15054
ISBN 0-8057-6645-6 (alk. paper)

Contents

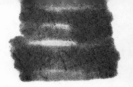

About the Author

Heather Arden earned her B.A. at Michigan State University (1965) and her M.A. and Ph.D. at New York University (1967, 1974). She has also studied in Paris and Strasbourg. Her dissertation, which examined the *sottie,* a type of late medieval comic play performed by fools or jesters, was published in 1980 by Cambridge University Press under the title *Fools' Plays: A Study of Satire in the Sottie.* While continuing to work on the late medieval theater, she has also moved back in time to study twelfth- and thirteenth-century French romance. In 1977 she participated in a National Endowment for the Humanities Summer Seminar on "Modern Approaches to Medieval Literature," led by Peter Haidu at the University of Illinois. Since then she has held a number of grants for research on medieval romance, including an American Council of Learned Societies Study Fellowship and a NEH Summer Stipend. She has served as the French editor of *Studies in Medievalism,* a journal devoted to studying the influence of medieval thought, art, and literature on later periods. After teaching at Wilkes College in Pennsylvania, in 1978 she came to the University of Cincinnati, where she teaches courses on medieval literature and on women in French literature.

Preface

The *Roman de la rose* was the best-known work in French from the thirteenth to the sixteenth century; it had a greater influence on medieval European literature than any work after Boethius's *Consolation of Philosophy*; it has come down to us in hundreds of manuscripts, many of them richly illuminated, the possessions of kings and lords. Yet today few people read it, even in translation, because it is a difficult work for modern readers to understand. I hope through this study to introduce the *Rose* to students at various levels, from beginners to graduate students to scholars in French or other European literatures who, knowing of the importance of the *Rose,* want a guide that will teach them more about it. For this reason I assume little or no previous knowledge of medieval French literature or of Old French on the part of the readers, and I translate all excerpts from the *Rose* in addition to summarizing it in some detail. Therefore, all readers need is the desire to become better acquainted with this landmark in European literature.

Medieval literature is today the subject of much lively and sophisticated critical discussion, and the *Rose* has benefited from this resurgence of interest in the Middle Ages. I can only point out in this study the importance of the scholarly debates, while trying to avoid polemics with scholars with whom I may disagree. Readers interested in pursuing these topics will find essential works listed in the bibliography.

One of the most important critical discussions in recent years centers on the supposed "alterity" (unavoidable otherness, differentness) of the Middle Ages. We recognize today that we cannot enter a medieval work as directly, as simply, as we can a modern work, that we have different presuppositions about what constitutes a work of literature than readers did in the medieval period. Since the *Rose* is in many ways a typical example of medieval French literature, our discussions of it will necessarily touch on many questions concerning the fundamental differences between medieval literature and modern. Thus, the reader will be helped to see medieval literature as a thirteenth- or fourteenth-century person may have responded to it. But I hope that this exercise in literary history will be followed by the reader's personal response to this challenging work. After exciting readers for over two hundred years, and then disappearing for three hundred, the *Rose* still has the power to challenge and entertain.

The first chapter presents what little information we have about the authors of the *Rose* (a work begun by Guillaume de Lorris and completed forty years later by Jean de Meun) and summarizes this enormous work in two ways, first through an outline, then through a fairly detailed synopsis. There is much humor in the *Rose,* despite its seemingly serious façade, and I hope that this summary reflects my own enjoyment of this humor. The chapter concludes with a discussion of the manuscripts and editions of the *Rose.*

The need to deal with a work of the length and complexity of the *Rose* prevented me from describing the general intellectual and social history of thirteenth-century France except as it directly affected the authors' ideas. Several good histories of the period are included in the bibliography for those who wish more information. However, an understanding of the philosophical and literary background of the *Rose* is essential. Therefore, the subject of the second chapter is the cultural traditions to which the authors of the *Rose* responded—writings on love, courtly or realistic; allegorical works from Prudentius to Bernard Sylvestris; dream literature, and, finally, the philosophical impact of thirteenth-century Aristotelianism.

Chapter 3 treats the text itself and the ways it uses allegory and personification. After modern theories of allegory are reviewed to help the reader understand this greatest of late medieval allegories, the chapter describes the larger allegorical patterns in the *Rose* and their poetic realization. The major personifications of the second part of the *Rose*—Reason, Nature, and Genius—are discussed in detail, and I offer a new interpretation of the literary status of Genius, the most enigmatic character of the *Rose* and the one that has caused the most critical controversy.

C. S. Lewis claimed in the *Allegory of Love* that the poems that derive from the *Rose* "constitute the most important literary phenomenon of the later Middle Ages." The enormous influence of the *Rose* on later writers is explored in chapter 4, especially on French writers of the fourteenth and fifteenth centuries, such as Guillaume de Machaut and François Villon, and on the Englishman Geoffrey Chaucer, the most important "disciple" of the *Rose*'s Art of Love. In attempting to assess the influence of the *Rose,* I also discuss various methods of determining influence and their drawbacks.

The critical ferment referred to earlier is the subject of the fifth chapter, which reviews the history of *Rose* criticism before the modern period and then analyzes and evaluates current critical approaches to the major problems that the *Rose* presents. The chapter will summarize some of the continuing debates on the *Rose,* such as the unity or opposition of the two parts. The complexity and ambiguity of the *Rose,* especially of Jean de Meun's continuation, have stimulated a variety of critical responses—the underlying message, for example, has been described both as pagan naturalism and as the most orthodox Christian theology. Therefore, I review the arguments made by the major schools of interpretation in order to clarify the critical assumptions of their proponents. Thus this discussion of an important work of medieval literature has the secondary goal of delineating the critical principles with which scholars today approach the Middle Ages.

The final chapter, the conclusion, stands back from the text and its critical history and attempts an overview of the *Rose,* especially the attitude that Jean de Meun expresses toward experience and authority. This chapter also suggests some reasons for its long popularity. What does it mean for our understanding of medieval literature that its most popular work, its *Gone with the Wind,* so to speak, is virtually inaccessible to most educated readers today? Does the *Rose* ask some fundamental questions that are still relevant today?

A French proverb says that the appetite increases while eating; I have found that the appetite for this rich, savoury, but difficult-to-digest work also grows through contact with it. I hope that this study of the *Rose* will encourage readers to go to the source.

A number of people have carefully and intelligently read this study in its various stages of "roughness." No doubt the errors remaining in the study, after such willing help, are mine. I particularly want to thank the following colleagues and scholars: Elizabeth Armstrong at the University of Cincinnati and Robert P. Miller, Professor Emeritus of SUNY Queens, for their helpful suggestions on the daunting subject of Chaucer and the *Rose*; Jeanne Nightingale, Taft Post-Doctoral Scholar at the University of Cincinnati, for her knowledgeable remarks on the allegorical tradition; Tom Kelly of Purdue University for help with the frontispiece, and the miniatures in general; and my French editor at Twayne, David O'Connell of the University of Illinois at Chicago. Paul Burrell read carefully the entire manuscript and led me into some thought-provoking discussions of what I was trying to get at. Our discussions are the most valuable part of my life at the university.

I also want to thank the Taft Fund and the University Research Council of the University of Cincinnati for their generous support and encouragement during the long process of writing this book.

Finally, for his patient and skillful editing of the entire manuscript, I thank my husband, Bruce Craddock.

Heather M. Arden

University of Cincinnati

Chronology

1270   Condemnation of the heterodox Aristotelian philosopher Siger de Brabant.

1265–1273   Saint Thomas Aquinas's *Summa theologiae.*

1277   Condemnation of the 219 heretical (mostly Averroïstic) theses by the bishop of Paris.

ca. 1280   *Il Fiore,* an Italian adaptation of the *Rose* in 230 sonnets.

1284   Jean de Meun translates *Epitoma rei militari* by Vegetius (fl. 385) as *L'Art de chevalerie.*

ca. 1360–1370   The *Remède de Fortune* and the *Dit de la fonteinne amoreuse* of Guillaume de Machaut.

1300–1311   Dante Alighieri's *Divine Comedy.*

before 1305   Death of Jean de Meun.

1387–1400   Geoffrey Chaucer's *Canterbury Tales.*

ca. 1390   Gower's *Confessio Amantis.*

ca. 1399–1402   The "Querelle de la Rose," a dispute over the literary merits and moral value of the *Rose.*

ca. 1460   François Villon's *Testament.*

ca. 1483   Jean Molinet's "moralized" prose version of the *Roman de la rose* (first printed 1500).

1526   Clement Marot's edition and modernization of the *Roman de la rose.*

Chapter One
The Authors and Their *Rose*

The *Roman de la rose* is an allegorical poem of 21,750 lines that tells the story of a dream in which a man falls in love, is separated from his loved one, suffers all the pains and tribulations of passion, and is rewarded in the end by being allowed to possess the one he loves. This most ordinary of plots needs thousands of lines for the telling and almost a hundred characters, for the *Roman de la rose* is no ordinary love story. Between the falling asleep and the awakening, many marvelous adventures and remarkable characters spring from the dreaming mind of the lover.

The Authors

The *Roman de la rose* was begun by Guillaume de Lorris in about 1225 and finished forty years later by Jean de Meun.[1] It is the God of Love himself who gives us in the romance the names of its authors: "Puis vendra Johans Chopinel" (l. 10535; then Jean Chopinel will come) to continue the story that Guillaume de Lorris began (see ll. 10496–648). The second author, Love tells us, will be born at Meun sur Loire, will serve the God of Love all his life, and will be such a wise man that he will not care a hoot about Reason. This is all the information that we have about the authors of the *Rose,* and it comes from one of the authors himself. In addition to their names and places of origin, we are told that Guillaume will die before finishing his work, that he wrote about forty years before Jean, and that Guillaume's part breaks off at a certain point (l. 4,028). We have no historical evidence to support these assertions, but they are generally accepted by scholars as true.

Since both authors came from the same province, it may have been there that Jean learned when Guillaume lived, and when he died. In any case, both Lorris and Meun (also spelled Mehun and Meung) are towns in the Orleanais, the province around Orleans. This is an old, prosperous province that is culturally rich and politically important in French history.

In Guillaume's account, he was about twenty years old when he had the dream that he is going to tell us: "El vintieme an de mon aage . . . vi un songe en mon dormant / qui mout fu biaus et mout me plot" (ll. 21, 26–27; In the twentieth year of my life, I saw a dream while sleeping that was very beautiful and pleasing).[2] Thus the poet had the dream just at the age when a young man's fancy turns to thoughts of love. That was about five years ago, he tells us, so he was about twenty-five when he began the *Rose*. Since Jean was born after Guillaume's death, he was a more mature man in his thirties when he began the continuation.

References to historical events and persons in the continuation have permitted scholars to establish an approximate date of composition between 1268 and 1285 (based on references to Manfred, Conradin, and Charles of Anjou). The first twentieth-century editor of the *Rose*, Ernest Langlois, narrows to 1275–80 the period during which Jean completed the work. Therefore, he believed that Guillaume stopped writing between 1225 and 1240.[3] Another editor, Felix Lecoy, places the date of the first part between 1225 and 1230 and of the second part between 1269 and 1278 (1:viii). In any case, we know the date of Jean's death, which occurred sometime before November 1305 (1:viii).

Both authors knew Latin and were familiar with classical authors, Jean to a much greater extent than Guillaume, who mentions only Macrobius, Alexander, Paris, and some gods and goddesses (drawn from Ovid's *Metamorphoses*). Langlois concludes from the fact that Guillaume refers to Scipio as a king that he was not a great scholar (*L*, 1:2). Jean, on the other hand, was probably a master of arts (he is referred to as "maistre" in the manuscripts) and gives evidence of wide classical learning. He refers to a variety of classical authors, historical figures, heroes, heroines, and divinities, including Aristotle (four times), Plato (nine times), Adonis, Ceres, Eneas, Minos, Cicero, Juvenal, Horace, and many others. His reading in the classics is as broad as that of a learned person in the Renaissance.

Jean names fewer theologians and fathers of the church than classical figures: only saints Peter and Paul, Origen, Boethius, and Abelard are mentioned. The questions that preoccupy the author of the continuation are for the most part not theological, and for this and other reasons I doubt that Jean had studied much beyond the master of arts level. In 1255, when all the works of Aristotle were put on the list of required reading at the Arts Faculty of the University of Paris, the unofficial policy of teaching Aristotle that had existed for at least two decades was made official. It is likely that Jean was a student in the Arts Faculty at this time, so he would have become familiar with Aristotle's philosophy without having to enter the School of Theology.

In addition to his part of the *Rose*, Jean made a number of translations from Latin to French. We still have three of them: *L'Art de Chevalerie (Epitoma rei militari)* of Vegetius, *La vie et les epistres de maistre Pierre Abelart et Heloïs sa fame* (the life and letters of Master Peter Abelard and Heloise his wife), and *Li livres de Confort,* a translation of *De consolatione philosophiae (The Consolation of Philosophy)* of Boethius (one of the writers who most influenced Jean's thought). Evidently two of his translations have been lost, *Les Merveilles d'Irlande (De mirabilibus Hiberniae* of Girard de Barri) and *Li Livre Aelred d'Esperituel Amistié* (Aelred de Rievaux's *De spirituali amicitia*; see 1:ix–x). Two other works are attributed to him by a number of manuscripts, but the authenticity of the attributions has not been established. These are a literary will, *Le Testament maistre Jehan de Meun,* and its supplement, *Le Codicile de Jean de Meun sur les VII articles de la foi.*[4]

Jean probably lived in Paris for much of his life. We know that he occupied, perhaps as tenant, a house at the end of the rue Saint-Jacques at least from 1292 (the house is no longer there, but a plaque marks the site). He was a student at the University of Paris during a period of great philosophical and political turmoil, and the *Rose* shows how ardently concerned he was with the questions being discussed, such as the role of the Mendicant Orders in the University. His work offers a unique insight into a particular man's view of some of the important intellectual issues of his time.

Summary of the *Roman de la Rose*

The following outline of the entire romance will help orient the reader in the longer summary and the critical discussions which follow.

Overview of the Roman de la Rose

(1) Prologue (ll. 1–20)

(2) The Dreamer Falls in Love

    (a) The Dreamer finds and explores the Garden (ll. 21–1422)

        (i) The paintings of undesirable people on the wall (ll. 139–460)

(ii) Nature complains that man does not do her bidding (ll. 18991–19304)

(b) Genius gives his sermon to the troups (ll. 19369–20673)
Full pardon is granted to everyone who serves Nature through procreation (ll. 19475–20652)

(c) The Fortress is taken (ll. 20653–21315)

(i) The story of Pygmalion (ll. 20786–21184)

(ii) Venus sends her torch into the tower (ll. 21221–246)

(d) The Lover possesses the Rose and awakens (ll. 21316–750)

Summary of the First Part of the *Roman de la rose*.   In a short prologue the poet claims that dreams tell us the good or the evil that will befall us and that what was at first unclear becomes clear later. Then the story begins. When the poet was twenty, he had a dream. Love commands him to tell us this dream, which he will call "li Romanz de la Rose / ou l'art d'Amors est tote enclose" (ll. 37–38; the Romance of the Rose, which contains all the art of love). May the one he loves accept it gladly.

In the merry month of May, when all the birds are singing, the poet dreams that he arises one morning, washes his hands and sews on his sleeves with a silver needle, and goes for a walk. Strolling happily along, he comes to a river, which he follows to an enclosed garden on whose walls are ten paintings of uncourtly vices: Hate, Felony, Villainy, Covetousness, Avarice, Envy, Sadness (Tristesse), Old Age (Vieillesse), Hypocrisy (Papelardie),[5] and Poverty. The singing of the multitude of birds in the garden is so beautiful that the narrator looks for a way to enter. A lovely blond maiden finally opens a little gate. She is Idleness (Oiseuse) and spends all her time getting ready to have fun and then having it. She is, of course, rich and noble.

Idleness tells the Lover that the garden belongs to Lord Merriment (Deduit),[6] and that every kind of tree grows there. His friends, who are as beautiful as angels, amuse themselves in what the narrator believes to be an earthly paradise: "Dex! com menoient bone vie!" he exclaims (l. 1293; God, what a good life they were leading!). Gaiety (Liesse) is singing to them as they dance in a circle: the ladies—Idleness, Beauty, Wealth (Richesse), Generosity (Largesce), Candor (Franchise), Courtesy, and Youth (Joinece)—are described in detail. Wealth receives the most attention (more lines than any other character, including the God of Love). An indication of her great wealth is the marvelous stone on her belt that cures toothache. The ladies are accompanied by their boy friends (who are not named), by Lord Merriment, and by the God of Love (Beauty's lover), who is dressed in a remarkable robe made entirely of flowers, while birds fly around his head. Accompanying him is Sweet Look (Douz Regart), who carries the God's two bows and ten allegorical arrows: Beauty, Simplicity, Candor, Companionship, Fair Seeming (Bel Samblant) (the qualities that promote love); Proudness (Orguelz), Villainy, Shame (Honte), Despair, and Fickle Thoughts (Noviaus Pensers) (those that destroy love).

While the Lover takes a tour of the garden, the God of Love follows him, bow in hand. The Lover arrives at a fountain under a pine that he recognizes as the fountain of Narcissus. The story is retold to serve as an example to the ladies not to be too proud toward their suitors. With some apprehension, the Lover approaches and peers into the fountain, where he sees two beautiful crystals. Each crystal reflects, like a mirror, half of the garden. In particular the Lover sees in them some rosebushes, so magnificent that he cannot help leaving the fountain and approaching them. In the bushes he sees one bud more beautiful than all the rest, and at this moment the God of Love begins to loose his arrows, striking straight to the Lover's heart through his eyes.

The God of Love now approaches the Lover, who, though he has pulled the shafts from his heart, will never be cured from the wounds of love. After taking the Lover as his vassal and locking his heart with a little golden key, the God of Love gives his commandments: (1) Avoid baseness (*vilenie*); (2) Do not speak evil of others; (3) Be courtly and agreeable; (4) Do not use vulgar words; (5) Serve and honor all women; (6) Avoid pride; (7) Dress elegantly; (8) Be ever joyful; (9) Do what will be enjoyable to others; and (10) Do not be avaricious. After summarizing his rules, the God of Love adds a definition of true love: Think only of love; Love only one person; Give your love entirely (not as a loan).

The Lover is next told that he will know the full measure of joy and pain if he will serve the God of Love faithfully: he will strive to be in the presence of the beloved, to whom he has sent his heart on ahead; he will "burn" when in her presence but will not be able to draw back; he will believe that he is holding her in his arms at night; he will grow thin and pale. To help him endure such wonderful suffering, the God of Love will send him Sweet Thoughts, Sweet Converse (a friend to whom he can talk), Sweet Look, and above all Hope. Then the God of Love leaves.

The Lover approaches the hedge that guards the roses but hesitates to cross it. Now there comes to his aid an important character named Warm Welcome, who represents the beloved in a friendly mood and who is the only one who can give the Lover what he wants. At the invitation of Warm Welcome, the Lover draws near the Rose, but as he reaches out to touch it, a horrible peasant named Resistance (Dangiers)[7] leaps out with his compagnons, Bad Mouth (Male Bouche), Shame, and Fear. (Shame is the daughter of Reason and the devil; her mother has sent her to help Chastity, the lady to whom the roses belong.) The Lover flees after Warm Welcome jumps over the hedge and disappears.

Just when the Lover believes that he is going to die of grief, he receives an important visit—Dame Reason descends from her tower to try to talk some sense into the young man. She who is supposedly greater and more powerful than Nature advises him to forget this madness, but when he angrily refuses, she withdraws.

At this low point, Friend arrives to advise the Lover. Resistance must be pacified and softened by assurances that the Lover wants only the right to love, not any physical reward. Candour and Pity help the Lover approach Resistance, who moderates his anger and allows Warm Welcome to rejoin the Lover. Warm Welcome leads the Lover by the hand into the presence of the beloved rosebud, who has become even more beautiful but who is still unopened (for which the Lover is happy). The Lover now goes one step further—he audaciously asks for a kiss. When Warm Welcome refuses from fear of Chastity, there suddenly appears Chastity's great enemy, Venus herself, to help the Lover. She manages to persuade Warm Welcome to grant the kiss, a kiss that fills the Lover with a joy that makes all the pain he has suffered worthwhile.

Now another and more serious setback occurs: Bad Mouth runs to Jealousy to tell her what has happened. Jealousy immediately orders a new wall to be built around the roses, with a tower in the center of the garden in which to imprison Warm Welcome. A guard is placed at each of the four doors of the tower and La Vieille, an old woman who knows all the tricks, is instructed to watch Warm Welcome. The Lover begins a long lamentation that the author will never finish—here ends the first part.

Summary of second part. The Lover, continuing his lamentation, becomes so despairing that he considers repenting his service to the God of Love. As he prepares his last will and testament, Reason returns to try again—this time she will speak for 3,000 lines (one seventh of the entire poem) in contrast to her earlier speech of 74 lines. Her first task is to make the Lover understand the nature of the love that he feels. She describes the God of Love in a long series of oxymorons ("desperate hope," "sweet suffering" ll. 4263–304); she defines love as a "maladie de pensée" (l. 4348); she points out that Youth is particularly susceptible to this disease and the vices that it inspires. Reason recognizes that procreation is so necessary that Nature has made it pleasurable, but he who looks only for pleasure enslaves himself to the "prince de trestouz les vices" (l. 4398; the prince of all the vices).

Alas, everything that Reason sends in one ear, the God of Love throws out the other! But at least the Lover is willing, this time, to have Reason explain the different types of human love that exist. This question sets off a long discourse on a variety of topics: friendship (the kind of love that Reason wants the Lover to follow); love for gain; how Fortune shows who real friends are; the true function of material possessions; love of one's fellowman (a more accessible love than true friendship); and the superiority of love over justice.

While discussing justice, Reason alludes to the myth of the castration of Saturn by Jupiter, his son. She drops in the word "coilles" (l. 5507; testicles), which so shocks the Lover—didn't the God of Love command him to avoid improper language?—that he pays no attention to the meaning of Reason's parable. Reason puts off her self-justification, because first she wants to show the Lover that to refuse passion does not mean to feel only hate. She wants him to feel the natural love for one's fellow creatures that even animals feel. But since she does not wish him to remain without an "amie," she offers herself in the place of the Rose. She asks only three things from the Lover: that he serve her loyally, that he leave the God of Love, and that he not give a prune for Fortune and her favors. Here Reason picks up again the subject of Fortune, which is one of the major themes of her discourse. To the hundreds of lines in which earlier she spoke of Fortune, she now adds a thousand more. Clearly this is one of the questions that most concerned Jean de Meun.

The major argument against Fortune is that it is not under our control. To convince the Lover of this, Reason resorts to all the techniques of medieval disputation: syllogisms, extended allegorical descriptions based on abstract concepts, examples drawn from mythology and even from current events, quotations from well-known authorities. Reason describes in 250 lines the House of Fortune, but stories of famous classical characters make up most of her discourse. For example, she recounts at length the fall of Nero and of Cresus. The Lover is referred to the example of Charles of Anjou, king of Sicily, if he prefers current events to ancient history, and the battle of Benevent (26 February 1266) is described as if it were a game of chess (chess has been described as resembling war, but has anyone before described war as a game of chess?).

Finally Reason returns to the three requests that she made earlier; she now argues that if the Lover feels that three are too great a burden she asks him to simply follow the first—if he accepts her as his beloved, the rest will follow automatically. Yet Reason's method of persuasion has been to convince the Lover only of the third proposition, that he should despise Fortune, as though the other two would follow from that, as though the passionate love that the God of Love inspires is one of the principle goods of Fortune. Consequently, before returning to the subject of dirty words, Reason throws in one last argument against her enemy, Fortune, that of the two barrels from which Jupiter pours happiness and misery to mankind (an image from Homer, *Iliad,* book 24).

Reason now explains why she spoke so bluntly earlier about sexual things: she may designate, by its proper name, anything that God her father created—and it certainly was he who created the instruments that sustain the human race. But, objects the Lover, if God made the things, he certainly did not make the words. So Reason claims the right, because she is reason, to speak clearly and directly of whatever she wishes. In any case, the names of things are arbitrary, she argues— if testicles were called "reliquaries," then "reliquaries" would be a dirty word. The Lover admits that he was wrong about her language, but that he is not wrong to wait for his reward from the God of Love: "je veill amer, conment qu'il aille, / la rose où je me sui voez" (ll. 7182–83; I want to love, whatever may come of it, the rose to which I have pledged myself). Reason gives up, once and for all, and goes off.

At this point Jean de Meun calls back Friend, who assures the Lover that he will rejoin Warm Welcome one day. In anticipation, then, of the Lover's winning of the Rose, Friend exposes—in a speech that is almost as long as Reason's (2,772 lines)—the best methods to overcome the guardians of the Rose and the way to keep the beloved once she has been won. Friend proposes a series of Machiavellian maneuvers to manipulate Bad Mouth, Jealousy, and the Old Woman: pretend that you do not care about Warm Welcome, that you have no bad feelings toward Bad Mouth and friends; give gifts to everyone (or promise to give); weep a lot; finally, if nothing else works, take the Rose by force. The Lover balks at such underhanded methods but is finally convinced to try them for Warm Welcome's sake.

But isn't there an easier way, he asks? Yes, the Road of Too Much Giving, Friend replies, but he does not recommend this path, for it leads to Poverty, the evils of which are described in several hundred lines. Poverty is seen as totally negative, except that it teaches you who your real friends are. Friend is here developing the ideas on wealth and fortune exposed earlier by Reason, by adding to her arguments (that true friendship is the greatest blessing that man can attain) the very words that a true friend might use. This technique of giving in direct discourse the words of a certain type of person will be used at great length in the second part of Friend's speech. Therefore, Friend concludes, to avoid poverty the Lover should only give inexpensive little gifts, such as fresh fruits or flowers.

Friend now turns to the topic of keeping a woman's love (this takes up two thirds of his speech). This section was one of the most controversial parts of the romance in the Middle Ages, for it includes the imagined tirade of the Jealous Husband—1,000 lines of the purest misogyny. This invective is preceded and followed by a discussion of the Golden Age as Friend imagines it (other characters will give us other versions). A denunciation of the avarice of women leads to a description of the sincere, loyal love that existed in the Golden Age. At that time people gathered their food rather than growing it, so fertile was the earth; everyone was equal, there was no private property or law; both lovers were equal because the love relationships followed the pattern of the social structure in which they were found. In any case, Friend argues, love and domination are always incompatible.

At this point the example of the Jealous Husband is introduced to show how a husband's desire to control his wife leads to the death of love. While making this point, Friend has the husband denounce his wife, marriage, and women in general (with many examples from history and mythology). The husband rejects artificial beauty and ornaments in favor of natural beauty: women who decorate themselves insult God. All women want is sex, anyway: "Toutes estes, serez et fustes, / de fet ou de volenté, pustes" (ll. 9125–26; All of you are, have been, and will be / In fact or thought, whores). But when the Jealous Husband tries to have a little fun, his wife claims she does not feel well! So the Jealous Husband insults not only his wife's imagined lovers but even his mother-in-law, who he claims is selling his wife! Finally, beside himself with rage, the Jealous Husband begins to beat his wife, and the neighbors rush in to pull him off.

Friend now returns to his account of the Golden Age. After a time the Vices arrive to attack the good people of the age, vices that include Poverty, Pride, and Avarice. Private property, government, arms, and general unhappiness are the result. At last Friend returns to his original topic—how to keep a woman's love—and he gives the Lover a series of rules of conduct (based on Ovid). Simply put, a man must allow a woman to do whatever she wants, never criticize her, and tell her continually how beautiful she is (even if she is declared ugly by everyone else). Having finished his discourse, Friend leaves the Lover to put his advice to the test.

Sweet Thought and Sweet Talk return, to encourage the Lover in his new approach to the Rose's guardians. While wandering near the castle, the Lover comes across Wealth, who blocks him from entering the Way of Too Much Giving (which Friend had already warned him against), and who describes in greater detail than Friend had done the consequences of following this path: Poverty awaits him, and Hunger (who lives near Scotland). Wealth, who hates all lovers because they do not keep the riches she gives them, chases the Lover away.

The God of Love returns to scold the Lover for having doubted— that is, for having listened to Reason. The Lover protests that he wants to live, and to die, serving the God of Love—in fact, he hopes that he will die in the act of love! After having him repeat his commandments, the God of Love forgives the Lover his moment of weakness and decides to summon his barons for an all-out attack on Jealousy's castle. Among the soldiers there appear two important new characters, False Seeming (Faus Semblant) and his girl friend, Forced Abstinence (Atenance Contrainte). The God of Love then addresses the troops: he exhorts them to do their best for the sake of the two authors who will write the account of this monumental conflict—he names Guillaume de Lorris and Jean Chopinel de Meung (who, he points out, has not been born yet) and claims that they will receive their deep understanding of love directly from the God himself.

The barons decide on a plan of attack: False Seeming and Forced Abstinence will attack Bad Mouth; Courtesy and Generosity, the Old Woman; Delight and Discretion, Fear: Openness and Pity, Resistance. The barons want to ask the help of Venus, but the God of Love claims that he cannot call on his mother whenever he feels like it. He condemns some of her activities, which involve buying love—an impossibility, since one cannot own a person like a horse. Wealth is scolded for having refused to join the combatants, and the God of Love promises to punish her by having his maidens fleece her wealthy followers.

Now the God of Love turns to False Seeming and asks him to tell them where he can be found in case of need: this deceptively simple question provokes an answer that goes on for a thousand lines. False Seeming is deception of any kind but especially the religious hypocrisy to be found in the Mendicant Orders, whose poverty is a sham. The author has False Seeming discuss several of the issues and events that were involved in the conflict of the secular and mendicant clerics at the University of Paris in the mid-thirteenth century. For example, False Seeming argues that every able-bodied man must work, even those who have taken orders; he gives details on the kind of schemes and plots that the mendicants use to grow rich and destroy their enemies; he discusses the *Evangelium aeternum* of Gerard de Borgo San Donnino and the efforts of Guillaume de Saint Amour to combat it. At times False Seeming broadens his remarks to point out that everyone, not only men of the church, must use hypocrisy and guile in order to succeed: his father Deception (Barat) is emperor of the world (ll. 11867–68). The God of Love is taken aback and does not know whether he can trust False Seeming to serve his cause. "Take a chance," replies the hypocrite, who firmly promises to use his methods in the service of love.

The attack begins. Disguised as pilgrims, False Seeming and Forced Abstinence approach Bad Mouth, who is sitting in front of his door, watching the world go by. Not suspecting anything, he welcomes the travelers and asks them for news. Forced Abstinence gives him instead a sermon in which she chastizes him for his slander of others, particularly of the Lover. He denies the charges; False Seeming proves that what she says is true; Bad Mouth kneels down to confess; False Seeming quickly cuts his throat and throws him in a ditch. Now the way is open to the tower in which Warm Welcome is held.

The two pilgrims, rejoined by Courtesy and Generosity, find the Old Woman strolling near the tower and, with sweet talk and gifts, persuade her to take a wreath of flowers to Warm Welcome as a token of esteem from the Lover, and to let him speak to the Lover. (But False Seeming thinks, and the Lover agrees, that if the Old Woman had not cooperated they would have found a way around her.) The Old Woman persuades Warm Welcome, with some difficulty, to accept the wreath. She praises the Lover hyperbolically, although as far as we know she does not know him (she expects a reward for her going-between): "il vos aime, n'en doutez mie, / de bone amor sanz vilenie" (ll. 12603–4; he loves you, never doubt it, with a good love in which there is no baseness). But before she brings the two young men[8] together, the Old Woman decides to instruct Warm Welcome in the ways of love (a lesson that will last almost 2,000 lines).

The Old Woman begins her speech with her credentials: she has had much experience in love because she was once very beautiful, but she did not profit by it, so now that she is old, ugly, and poor, she wants Warm Welcome to take revenge on men for her by fleecing his suitors. At this point the narrator interjects a curse on the Old Woman for teaching Warm Welcome how to deceive him. Now the games of love are described in a way that is as cynical as it is thorough. First of all, Warm Welcome must ignore the last two rules of the God of Love—to love only one person, and to love that person completely. "Do not *give* your heart, says the Old Woman, *sell* it" (ll. 13010–12). And promise the Rose to everyone: The gods forgive lovers for breaking their vows, for the gods themselves do it all the time. She then gives examples of unfaithful lovers: Eneas, Demophon, Paris, Jason. All men are deceivers, proclaims the Old Woman, in a statement that parallels the Jealous Husband's condemnation of women for their lechery (ll. 13235–38).

But how to acquire the charms that will attract the poor fools? The Old Woman's answer includes advice on physical beauty and hygiene, on table manners, on how to walk in public, even on what to do if a woman has bad breath or breasts too large. Then, once she has attracted a suitor (avoiding the poor, the traveler, and the vain), she must know how to fleece him to the last *sou*. At this point the Old Woman interjects a version of the legend of how Venus and Mars were caught in Vulcan's net, a story that is interrupted by another aside in which the Old Woman proclaims that all people are born free to love as often and whomever they wish—and this is particularly true of women. She gives examples first of how precious liberty is, then of how all creatures must obey the force of Nature.

After concluding the story of Venus with the moral that a woman caught in the act will then do openly what before she concealed, the Old Woman continues her instruction in how to manipulate men. Make them wait (impatience whets the appetite), frighten them with cries that the husband is returning (fear whets the appetite), pretend to enjoy the same sexual pleasure as they do (simultaneity whets the appetite). Finally, the Old Woman instructs her patient pupil with advice on overcoming a too vigilant husband and on the kind of gifts a woman may give a man ("Don't be too generous"). She then gives in to regrets at having wasted her youth, that is, at having given away all that she received from her suitors to the man she loved—a scoundrel who would take her money, beat her, and run off to the tavern. May Warm Welcome profit from her example.

Warm Welcome, skeptical of the Old Woman's approach to love but reassured by her that she will take care of Jealousy should she return unexpectedly, agrees to speak with the Lover. The Old Woman sends the Lover in by the back door, where Sweet Look leads him to Warm Welcome. On his way, the Lover has passed the massed hosts of the God of Love (including Forced Abstinence who has gotten herself pregnant by False Seeming; she will give birth to the Antichrist). The Lover appears to misunderstand Warm Welcome's polite remark that everything he has is the Lover's too, and he reaches out his hand to the Rose. Once again the enemies of love are ready—Resistance leaps out from his hiding place and shouts, "Flee, flee, flee, flee" (ll. 14797–98)! He is joined by Shame and Fear, and the three scold the Lover and imprison Warm Welcome behind a triple lock. When the Lover begs them to put him in the prison cell with Warm Welcome, they start to beat him. He cries for help, softly, and the barons of Love rush up to save him.

At this suspenseful moment, the author stops the action (of which there has been so little) to speak to his readers. He wants to excuse and justify himself in three respects: he defends himself against the charges of having used obscene language, of having criticized "les moeurs fe-menins" (l. 15196; feminine manners), and finally of having attacked religious men through his description of False Seeming.

Now the battle can begin. A series of hand-to-hand combats takes place, as in medieval epics. Each soldier is first described in terms of the allegorical arms, especially the shield and sword, that he or she carries. Candour is defeated by Resistance, but Pity rushes up and softens him by flooding him with tears. Shame attacks furiously and forces Pity to pull back. Pleasure (Deliz) throws himself on Shame, but she defends herself very well until Discretion hits her so hard that he half kills her. Fear, normally very timid, is so angry that she attacks Discretion, who calls on Bravery, who is knocked down by Fear. Safety tries to overcome Fear but fails.

The battle is going badly for the forces of the God of Love. He quickly arranges a truce and sends a messenger to bring his mother, Venus, who is dallying with Adonis on Cytherea. She asks him not to chase the big beasts, just the rabbits and such; he promises hypocritically, and is killed by a boar. The moral: "Lords, believe your lady friends, for their words are as true as history" (l. 15726). Venus has her chariot harnessed with six doves and arrives at the battle field, where her son has already broken the truce by hurling rocks of Prayers and arrows of Promises. The God of Love pronounces a long condemnation of men who refuse the service of love—they are not real men: "Ou peut l'an querre meilleur vie / que d'estre antre les braz s'amie?" (ll. 15845–46; Where can one find a better life than between the arms of one's lover?)

. While the God of Love and his mother are swearing to destroy Chastity, the scene suddenly changes: we see before us a new character, Nature, sitting by her forge and lamenting. Her lamentation and confession, which last for over 3,000 lines, constitute one of the major sections of the romance. Nature begins by describing how Death sooner or later captures every living creature, but he cannot destroy the species because he cannot catch everyone at once. Nature, by forging new individuals, defeats Death. Art, the ape of Nature, has been watching her work and begging for her secrets but cannot make living things. Alchemy, although a true art, can change individuals but not species. Nature, however, is not happy. She felt momentarily better when she heard the oath of Venus and Love, but she is still so sad that she wants to confess to her priest, Genius. (The author has refused to try to describe Nature, and he lists those who have already failed. He will say, however, that she is the fountain from which all beauty flows.)

Genius makes ready to hear her confession, but first he asks her to stop crying. Rather than letting Nature begin, Genius gives her a little sermon—400 lines of severe criticism of women. They have many faults, but one of the most serious is that they cannot keep a secret. Many a husband has been undone because he allowed himself to tell his wife something that could be used against him. And Genius treats us to an imagined conversation between a wife and husband in bed at night. "Protect yourself from women" is his advice to men (l. 16547; "gardez vos de fames"), but honor and serve them long enough to continue your species. He assures Nature that he did not say all that for her sake, for she is endlessly wise.

Nature's "confession" begins. She reviews all the parts of the universe to show that each is doing its duty toward God and Nature, God's vicar, except one creature, Man. God created the universe *ex nihilo* only because of his generous will, and everything has been perfectly ordered. Most of Nature's description deals with the heavens (2,250 lines); plants and animals will be mentioned in a few lines at the end. This cosmology is interrupted at several points in order for Nature to correct two common, but serious, errors: she proves that free will and divine omniscience are not incompatible; she describes the true nobility that comes from virtue, not the false nobility of social status. This long section also includes a discussion of optics, visions and hallucinations, the belief that comets signify the death of kings, and a description of a flood.

Finally Nature voices her complaint about man: he is the only part of the universe who rebels against her. She has given him greatness (although she admits her limits: only God gives him understanding), but has he shown his gratitude by obeying Nature's laws? No, man has instead indulged in every possible vice, but when he appears before his Judge he will be sent to hell and Nature will be vindicated. It is of his sexual misdeeds that Nature complains most bitterly, and she sends Genius to speak to the followers of Love, to excommunicate those who refuse natural procreative love. But to those who do their duty by her, she grants full pardon forever.

Genius arrives in the camp of the God of Love, whose soldiers give him a joyous welcome. After putting on the vestments of a bishop, he pronounces his "diffinitive santance," a sermon that will last for over a thousand lines. This speech has two major sections: an exhortation to pursue procreative sex and a description of the heavenly garden that awaits good procreators. In developing his theme that those who love well will go to heaven, Genius uses three metaphors for intercourse: the stylus writing on a tablet, a hammer forging on an anvil, and a plow ploughing a fertile field. After a long diatribe against homosexuality, Genius urges the barons of love to defeat Atropos (who is continually destroying men) by making more men. He urges them to preach this "virtuous and precious" message to the world.

To encourage his followers, Genius gives them a long description of the "parc du champ joli" of the blessed souls (l. 19905; the garden of the beautiful meadow). This paradise is described in religious terms, despite the fact that those who will enter have chosen not to take the church's preferred road of chastity and continence (there is no mention of marriage). Nonetheless, all the inhabitants of the garden are described as little white lambs whose shepherd is Christ.

In this garden we find the fountain of life rather than "la fontaine périlleuse" (the perilous fountain) of the God of Love; three waters flow from it rather than two, and they join into one stream; near it grows an olive tree that bears the fruit of salvation. Genius makes frequent comparisons between this wondrous, eternal garden and the falsely alluring, transient garden of Lord Merriment. Then he throws his candle into the assembly, thereby setting all the women in the world on fire. Everyone cries "Amen," and Genius disappears.

Venus takes command of the army and the final assault begins. She calls on her adversaries to surrender, but when they arrogantly refuse, she threatens to give Chastity's roses to everyone, both clerics and laymen. Now a new obstacle appears in the Lover's path: Venus sees a little loophole (a narrow window in a fortification from which one can shoot arrows) between two ivory pillars. On top of the pillars is a statue of a beautiful woman in the form of a reliquary. The description of the statue leads to a long retelling (400 lines) of the story of Pygmalion and his statue, which was brought to life by Venus. As the Lover, dressed as a pilgrim, follows the road toward the "shrine" of the statue, Venus sends a flaming arrow into the tower, and the guards all flee. Courtesy, Pity, and Candour save Warm Welcome from the fire. At last Warm Welcome gives the Rose to the Lover.

Before plucking his rose, however, the Lover must first pass by the statue-shrine. On his way, the Lover describes women as narrow ways or broad roads and speculates on the advantages of having a rich old mistress. Provided by Nature with a large staff and a pouch (which contains two hammers "for shoeing his horse," the Lover wryly claims), he is now prepared to touch the relic in the shrine. But when he inserts his staff in the loophole, he finds that something is obstructing the passageway. He must try again and again to force his staff in—working as hard, he exclaims, as Hercules. At last he succeeds, but the pouch remains hanging outside. He believes that he is the first person to pass through the shrine (though he wonders if he will be the last), but it was the only way to the Rose.

Finally the Lover takes hold of the rosebush and plucks the Rose, excusing himself for having broken the bark a little and for having spilled a little of the seed. The Lover thanks those who helped him, curses those who opposed him, and, rather abruptly, awakes: "Ainsint oi la rose vermeille. / Atant fu jorz, et je m'esveille" (ll. 21749–50; Thus I had the vermillion rose. Then it was day, and I awoke). And thus too ends the *Roman de la rose.*

Manuscripts and Editions

The manuscripts of the *Roman de la rose* are both numerous (an indication of the romance's popularity) and richly illustrated. In 1910, the first specialist in the study of the *Rose*, Ernest Langlois, cataloged 215 manuscripts and attempted to classify 116.[9] Felix Lecoy added thirty-two and suggested that others may still exist (1:xxxv–xxxvi). Therefore, the number of known manuscripts, not counting fragments, is at least 247. While this is less than half of the manuscripts still preserved of the *Divine Comedy* (600), it is many more than the manuscripts of Chrétien de Troyes's *Lancelot* (six), of the *Canterbury Tales* (84), or of *Sir Gawain and the Green Knight* (one).

All the manuscripts but one are made up of both parts of the romance. The one exception gives the first part followed by a short, not very interesting, completion (not related to Jean de Meun's). Evidently a large number of copies of part one existed when Jean de Meun's continuation appeared, and the second part was simply added to a preexisting copy of the first part (see Lecoy's discussion: 1:xxxvii–xxxviii). All of the existing manuscripts, again except one, are copies of texts that already contained both parts. Therefore, we do not have a copy of the first part dating from the period of composition. The texts of the second part are less corrupted than those of the first part.

Langlois's classification of a number of *Rose* manuscripts has been criticized by Lecoy for arbitrariness and incompleteness (1:xxxvii), but he has helped us to sort out the better manuscripts. Unfortunately, Langlois does not discuss the miniatures (he simply indicates in some cases whether they exist or not), but other scholars have begun to analyze the iconography of the manuscripts. Thomas Kelly and Thomas Ohlgren, for example, have begun an iconographic index of the *Rose* manuscripts in the Bodleian Library at Oxford.[10] A few scholars, such as John V. Fleming and Rosamond Tuve, have used the miniatures to help interpret the text.[11]

The *Rose* lends itself to illustration because of the topics discussed, the examples taken from classical mythology, and the scenes and characters presented. This may explain in part the popularity of the *Rose* in the Middle Ages, at least as a work to be collected by wealthy amateurs of beautiful books.[12] A number of the manuscripts have beautifully executed, richly illuminated miniatures, which tell us something of what medieval artists and scribes, and probably their public, too, considered to be important in the romance. The miniatures often show us, for example, the narrator dressed as a cleric when he begins his adventure but transformed into an elegant young gentleman when he falls in love. Certain episodes are singled out for illustration because they were of particular interest—nearly all manuscripts portray the Jealous Husband beating his wife and Pygmalion carving his statue.

The *Rose* was taken up by many of the early printers, and twenty-one editions were published between 1481 and 1538. F. W. Bourdillon has given us a thorough study of these early editions.[13] After 1538 interest in the *Rose* faded, and two centuries passed before another edition appeared—in 1735, Lenglet du Fresnoy published his three-volume edition, which was, however, unreliable. The first good edition of the *Rose* was brought out by M. Méon in 1814 (see chapter 5 below). Two major editions—by Ernest Langlois and Felix Lecoy—have been published in the twentieth century. Although they follow different principles of editing medieval texts, both editions are useful; Lecoy's edition is now used by most scholars.

Chapter Two
Literary and Philosophical Traditions

The *Roman de la rose* is evidently the first work in European literature to combine a love quest, an art of love, an allegory, and a dream vision. By blending preexisting elements Guillaume de Lorris created a romance that brought to its peak the courtly conception of love and offered to later medieval writers the allegorical means to express all their concerns—psychological, literary, and philosophical. Half a century later Jean de Meun built on this base a work that incorporated the principal philosophical and literary traditions of his time. In this chapter we will survey the many influences and traditions that contributed to this remarkable work.

Medieval Conceptions of Tradition and Originality

When we read a medieval work today, we bring to it certain assumptions concerning literary creativity—we generally expect to find originality, sincerity, intensity, and unity. This view of what a literary work should be is largely the result of attitudes that developed during the growth of the novel, from the Renaissance through romanticism, and therefore were not concerns of medieval writers. Until recently scholars were led to make pejorative judgments of medieval literature because they accepted these assumptions, but in order to understand a medieval work on its own terms, we must look for evidence of what a literary work meant in the Middle Ages, and especially, since we want to understand the *Roman de la rose,* in the thirteenth century.

A medieval author tried to create a pleasing work by reshaping into a more beautiful form materials found in other works. Neither medieval authors nor their public thought about "originality" in the sense we do today, that is, as the creation of a work that does not take ideas or language directly from another work (even the idea that authors "owned" their works did not develop until the eighteenth century).

Therefore, a medieval author claimed to have read the story he or she is telling in a book, although this was probably not true. What was valuable was not what an individual could create spontaneously but how he or she transformed material handed down by tradition. Even the authors whom we consider the most modern, Villon or Rabelais, for example, were reshaping traditional materials.[1]

When an author writes in a traditional form, we assume that he or she is not being "sincere," a quality that we look for in modern works (which are, in reality, as arranged and unspontaneous as medieval works). To a medieval author, the question of sincerity never arose—a work of art was expected to be a beautiful refashioning of received elements, not an outpouring of personal views and feelings. Furthermore, the fact that traditional images are used to express a view of love does not mean that the author did not experience love, merely that the question of sincerity is beside the point in appreciating the artistry that goes into the work. Therefore, it is not relevant to our reading of the *Roman de la rose* to ask whether Guillaume de Lorris "really" felt the feelings he described. The work must stand on its own.

Finally, the *Roman de la rose* and other medieval works have been criticized for their lack of unity, an aesthetic principle that came back into vogue in France in the seventeenth century through a reinterpretation of Aristotle's *Poetics*. Not only are many medieval works episodic in structure, but the episodes also combine elements from different traditions. This means that medieval works differ from many modern ones but not that they have no organizing principles. The unity and harmony of the cosmic order, for example, was seen as a model to be imitated in literary works. In the next chapter we will talk about how the various themes in the *Rose* are organized.

All this is a necessary prelude to the discussion that follows in order to show that the *Rose* is not worth less because it adapts medieval literary and philosophical traditions, and that we need to understand this unique reworking of tradition. In many ways the *Rose* is both the culmination of the major traditions of the Middle Ages and the beginning of new traditions. It is the first part of this process that we will look at in this chapter.

Classical and Medieval Writings on Love

Love in the first part of the *Rose*. The conception of love expressed by Guillaume de Lorris has been called "courtly love" by modern scholars. There has been considerable debate over the meaning and critical usefulness of the term in the past decade, for medieval literature generally does not refer to *amour courtois,* a term coined by the French scholar, Gaston Paris, in 1883.[2] But medieval writers do talk about *fin' amors,* refined, noble love. Whichever term is used, however, most scholars believe that new views of love developed in France in the eleventh and twelfth centuries. Medieval poets and romancers talk about love as an ennobling experience, the most valuable that life can give, and they express joy in their suffering (love is referred to as "li doux mal," the sweet pain). The first outstanding English scholar of the *Rose,* C. S. Lewis, believed that this new kind of love was of earth-shaking importance: "Compared with this revolution the Renaissance is a mere ripple on the surface of literature."[3] This is the kind of love that the Lover experiences in the first part of the *Roman de la rose.*

This new view of love had gone through three stages by the time it reached Guillaume de Lorris. It began at the end of the eleventh century in southern France and was expressed in the songs of the troubadours (the poets who wrote in Provençal), the most famous of whom were William IX of Aquitaine (the grandfather of Eleanor of Aquitaine) and Bernart de Ventadour. William is often referred to as the first troubadour because we have no record of an earlier poet. He has left us eleven songs, four of which are considered "courtly."[4] Bernart de Ventadour rose from obscurity (he was said to be the son of a kitchen wench) to fame as one of the best of the troubadours, a favorite of Eleanor of Aquitaine. Altogether there are songs from 460 troubadours in existence today, songs composed by a variety of men and women, both noble and commoner.[5] The themes and to some extent the forms of the *canso,* the *jeu parti,* and other Provençal lyrics were taken up and developed by northern French poets (called *trouvères*) in the twelfth and thirteenth centuries.

Several important themes in courtly songs recur in the first part of the *Rose.* The main theme of the songs is the lover's simultaneous feelings of great joy and great suffering. "I die of grief a hundred times a day / and a hundred times revive with joy," sings Bernart de Ventadour; "This pain is worth more than any pleasure." Jaufré Rudel alludes to the rose to express his feelings: "far more piercing than a thorn / is the pain only joy can cure."[6] The grief comes from two kinds of obstacles that separate the lover from the beloved (for in the courtly lyric there are always obstacles), either social barriers due to her status which is higher than the lover's, or barriers set up by the aloofness or coldness of the lady herself.

The beloved is of course the most perfect creature that Nature ever created: "I love the best and most beautiful," proclaims Bernart.[7] In the *Rose* the God of Love points out that one look from her is worth more than all the favors of another (ll. 2472–73; see also ll. 1655–58). This marvelous lady's favor (not her love, which the lover dare not even hope for) must be won by long and humble service: "Surely no one can ever be Love's / perfect man unless he gives it homage in humility."[8] So will the Lover in the *Rose* try to loyally serve the God of Love, through all the torments he suffers, in the hope of being granted life's greatest joy.

We find in the *Rose* many of the descriptive motifs that also appear in the lyric poems, such as the descriptions of the beauty of spring and the songs of the birds with which many poems begin. The songs offer Ovidian images of the arrows of love, of love as a fire, and they refer to classical myths such as that of Narcissus. Finally, many songs make feelings or abstract ideas into objects or forces acting on the poet with a seemingly independent force. Pity becomes, for Bernart, the key that will open the "prison" in which love has put him,[9] just as Pity softens up Resistance in the *Rose*.

We find the second stage of the evolution of courtly love in the romances of the twelfth century, in which love is celebrated in narrative as well as lyrical mode. Unlike antiquity, the Middle Ages made love the preeminent theme of narrative literature: love was at last taken seriously.[10] This new importance of love as a subject of storytelling can first be seen in a group of works called the *romans d'antiquité* (the novels of antiquity), works that are free adaptations of Greek or Roman history and mythology: the romances of Thebes and Troy, of Aeneas and Alexander, among others. Not only are love stories inserted into poems concerned mainly with military prowess, but the love-struck hero and heroine indulge in long monologues that express all the internal strife, doubts, hopes, and sufferings that love causes them.

The Arthurian romances of the second half of the twelfth century pick up and develop these two elements, the lovers' monologues and the importance of love to the plot. Chrétien de Troyes's *Lancelot* (ca. 1180) is the first romance to tell the adventures of the knight who came to represent the perfect courtly lover. In Chrétien's version, Lancelot undergoes many trials and torments before being brought into Guenevere's presence; she rejects him because he showed a moment of

weakness earlier; he undergoes more trials and torments that lead at
last to a night of love with Guenevere; they are separated by more trials
and torments but are finally reunited. Guillaume has followed the same
pattern of approach, separation, first union, separation, and final union
in the *Rose,* but he has put aside the external adventures in order to
play out the quest for love in the minds of the lovers. In this way all
the battles, setbacks, and trials in the *Rose,* therefore, have become
psychological ones.

Many twelfth-century French romances include lovers' monologues
in which feelings are described almost as though they were entities
separate from the lover. The most famous example of this tendency
toward personification is found in *Lancelot,* in that moment of weakness
for which Lancelot will later be rebuked: the author portrays the conflict in the hero's mind as a debate between Love and Reason. Charles
Muscatine, who analyzed the techniques of these monologues in "The
Emergence of Psychological Allegory in Old French Romance," found
in the fourteen romances studied an equivalent for every personification
in Guillaume de Lorris's *Rose* except Warm Welcome, Venus, and Jealousy.[11] It is this "romance matrix that puts the fictional (as opposed to
the didactic) stamp on the *Roman de la Rose.*" Furthermore, Muscatine
claims that though some in the medieval audience may have known
allegorical works like Prudentius's *Psychomachia,* they could not have
understood Guillaume's romance if they had not also been familiar with
the psychological allegory found in the romances of adventure.[12]

The third major phase through which courtly love passed was a tendency to codify its variable, fluctuating elements, to formulate a code
of behavior for the courtly lover. The most important attempt at cod-
ification was the late-twelfth-century *De arte honeste amandi (The Art of
Courtly Love,* also called *De amore,* On love) of Andreas Capellanus, an
"art of love," or rather seduction, in the tradition of the *Ars Amatoria
(The Art of Love* by the Roman poet Ovid [43 B.C.–17 A.D.]; this work
is discussed in the next section).[13] We know little about Andreas Capellanus (André le Chapelain in French); he may have been a chaplain
at a noble or royal court and probably knew Marie, countess of Cham-
pagne (the woman for whom Chrétien de Troyes wrote his *Lancelot*).

In the three books of the *De amore,* the author instructs a young man
in the ways to win a woman's love, to keep that love, or to stop loving
if he wishes. There are many similarities between this *Art of Courtly
Love* and Guillaume's romance (and even Jean de Meun's), and while
we are uncertain if both authors knew the work, it was likely they did,

for as late as 1277 it was still a *cause célèbre* and was condemned by the University of Paris.

Like the *Rose, The Art of Courtly Love* shows us the God of Love in a beautiful garden, the center of which is called "Delightfulness" and where we find a *fons* (spring or fountain). Here the knights and ladies who serve Love spend eternity: "No human tongue could tell how great was the blessedness and the glory of these people, for the whole place of Delightfulness was appointed for their pleasure. . . ."[14] And here the God of Love, like Guillaume's God, gives his commandments to the lover.[15] The rules given by the God of Love in book 1, fifth dialogue, generally follow the same pattern as those in the *Rose* (ll. 2073–2252; Andreas gives two longer but similar sets of instructions in book 1, third dialogue, and book 2, chapter 8). As in the *Rose,* the rules guide the lover in his relations with others and with the beloved in particular, they condemn certain vices (avarice, falsehood) and urge certain virtues (modesty), and they tell the lover to watch his tongue; Andreas's god, however, does not stress the personal qualities that interested Guillaume—good humor, a willingness to show off one's talents, and elegant dress. Nonetheless, *The Art of Courtly Love* was part of the tendency toward didacticism that marks parts of the *Rose.*

Book 1 of *The Art of Courtly Love* uses the framework of a series of conversations between a suitor and the woman he is trying to seduce (both are characterized mainly by their social rank) to develop a series of debates on various abstract questions of love—Which should one follow, one's heart or one's head? Should one reject a lover who lives too far away? The lover attempts to win the lady's love through persuasion: "I shall prove to you that you cannot properly deprive me of your love."[16] This aspect of Capellanus's work is closer to the Scholastic spirit of Jean's part, but even in the first part of the *Rose* Guillaume suggests the conflict of different views of love in the speeches of Reason and the Friend. Rather than engage his lovers in rational debate, Guillaume chooses to have his personifications act out the tug of war both within a person's mind and between a lover and his beloved. Both the *Rose* and the *The Art of Courtly Love,* however, agree that love is a world apart, an "order," with its own validity, its own values, independent of those of religion or society.

In addition to these courtly works, scholars have proposed, as possible influences on the first part of the *Rose,* a number of twelfth-century Latin works that present a noncourtly view of love. These works include the *Concile de Remiremont* (an untitled work; Langlois gives it this French title), the *Altercatio Phyllidis et Florae*, and especially the *Pamphilus*, a poem in 780 lines that was widely read in the Middle Ages. It tells of the seduction of a young woman by a young man, Pamphilus, who is aided by Venus and an Old Woman. Langlois argues at length that Guillaume was directly influenced by the *Pamphilus*, but his arguments are unconvincing, for the similarities could easily come from the fact that both authors drew from Ovid, and the differences in tone and point of view are striking.[17] Although these earlier works show that many twelfth- and thirteenth-century authors were thinking along similar lines when they wrote about love, none of these works presents the crucial combination of elements that we find in Guillaume's *Rose*.

Love in the second part of the *Rose*. Jean de Meun draws on two important sources of medieval thinking about love, Ovid's *Art of Love*, and the long tradition of misogynistic works that goes back to the time of Aristotle. An "art of love" is a literary work that may be either an instruction manual or a comprehensive treatise on all kinds of love. Ovid's three-part seduction manual is the most important example of the first kind of "art of love." It was basic reading in medieval schools and influenced not only both parts of the *Rose* but nearly all medieval works on love. Chrétien de Troyes made a translation of it that has been lost, but other translations existed in Guillaume's day. Guillaume de Lorris also refers to his work as an "art of love" (l. 38); like Ovid's, it is of the first kind (a seduction manual), for he is almost exclusively concerned with a man's love for a woman, while Jean's part expands the question into a consideration of other kinds of love. Guillaume, however, appears to recommend seriously the same behavior which Ovid recommends ironically.[18]

Medieval thinking on love was influenced not only by Ovid's *Art of Love* but by many of his other works, especially the *Amores*, short poems about an amorous liaison; the *Remedia amoris* (Love's remedy), the ways to cure oneself emotionally and physically of love; and the *Metamorphoses*, an enormous collection of ancient myths and stories, many dealing with love relationships. Ovid was the most widely read Latin author in the twelfth and thirteenth centuries, despite the concern of some theologians who denied the moral value of his works for Christians.[19] Both Guillaume and Jean borrowed from Ovid, Jean much more so than Guillaume, who took little more than his descriptions of a lover's sufferings from Ovid's *Art of Love*, and from the *Metamorphoses* the portrait of Envy, the motif of Love's arrows, and the legend of Narcissus (which Guillaume drastically reinterprets).[20]

Of these works Jean draws most often on the *Art of Love,* especially in the speeches of the Friend and the Old Woman. Using book 2 of Ovid's handbook, the Friend instructs the Lover, cynically and in detail, in how to keep his beloved once he has won her love (evidently he knows how the romance will end!). The Old Woman paraphrases book 3 in order to teach Warm Welcome how to profit by her charms. She also picks up sections of book 2, which was meant for men, and urges Warm Welcome, a woman, to use the same tactics (see ll. 13089–108). Jean does not draw on book 1 since it deals with how to win the woman you love—and Jean knows that his Lover will not take an active part in winning the Rose, that she will be handed to him by others, especially by Venus.

Ovid's advice is cynical and mildly misogynistic: "Any woman can be seduced; it is hard for a woman to burn for only one man; every woman believes herself beautiful, no matter how ugly she may be; in general, women are an unscrupulous race." At several points Jean's characters express these opinions and similar ones found in the standard misogynistic works that medieval authors drew on and that were developed with fervor in the third book of Andreas Capellanus's *Art of Courtly Love.* One of the earliest classical works in the misogynistic tradition is a satire on marriage by Theophrastus, a disciple of Aristotle. The Greek text has been lost, but excerpts from it were given to the Middle Ages in Saint Jerome's *Adversus Jovinianum* (Against Jovinian). Theophrastus draws a horrifying picture of marriage for a disciple who is thinking of marrying, an action that will end any hope of the contemplative life that a philosopher needs. Saint Jerome applies this point of view to a similar but Christian end, the higher virtue of virginity over marriage. In another work, the *Contra Helvidium* (Against Helvidius), Saint Jerome used the same arguments to persuade young women of the value of chastity. (Heloise used Saint Jerome's arguments to try to dissuade Abelard from marrying her.)

But Theophrastus and Saint Jerome do not limit their arguments to this theme of the *molestiae nuptiarum,* the troubles of marriage, for both authors also include attacks on women in general. In the twelfth century John of Salisbury, the secretary of Thomas Beckett, incorporated their arguments into book 8, chapter 11, of his *Policraticus* (1159). It was probably through John of Salisbury's version that Jean de Meun became familiar with the misogynistic themes that he used in the Friend's speech and in the tirade of the Jealous Husband in particular. Thus, Jean is receiving Theophrastus's ideas third or fourth hand (see ll. 8531–8802; 2:272–73).

The other major source of misogynistic arguments for medieval writers was the Latin satirist, Juvenal. His sixth satire is also addressed to a young man who is thinking of marrying: Why marry, when there are so many ropes to hang yourself with, so many windows to leap out of? The author regrets the good old days when women were chaste (though ugly, it seems); since then female vices have proliferated, and Juvenal proves his case by drawing the portraits of many kinds of women, who are in turn vicious, silly, naive, or arrogant. But they all share the desire to dominate their husbands, a trait with which Jean de Meun is also concerned. Many of Juvenal's remarks about women in satire 6, and to a lesser degree satire 7, will be worked into the Friend's speech as well as that of the Jealous Husband.

Literature satirizing women in both Latin and French continued throughout the Middle Ages—in the fabliaux and farces, most of which tell of wives' adultery; in collections of tales such as the *Cent nouvelles nouvelles* (A hundred new tales; fifteenth century); in antimarriage literature, such as the *Lamentations* of Matheolus (1295) and the fifteenth-century *Quinze Joyes de Mariage* (The fifteen "joys" of marriage). Early in the fifteenth century there was also a reaction against these works, a defense of women led by a woman, discussed in chapter 4 below, where I consider the influence of the *Rose* on later literature.

Allegorical Works

The medieval understanding of allegory as a literary medium was based largely on certain works from late antiquity, although allegorical thinking is of course much older. The works of Homer, for example, were interpreted allegorically by the second century B.C. and probably earlier. Latin authors used allegory and personification even more than the Greeks: Vergil's *Aeneid,* the *Thebaid* of Statius, and the *Wedding of Honorius and Marie* by Claudian present personified abstractions of passions and natural evils and were widely read in the Middle Ages. Although these works contributed to the development of medieval allegory, the most important contribution was made by three other Latin poems.

In the early fifth century, Prudentius gave Western literature the "earliest construction of an entire narrative from personified agents."[21] His *Psychomachia* is an epic battle between good and evil forces for a human soul and for the victory of Christianity over paganism and heresy. Prudentius's work differs from previous allegorical approaches because the characters behave like people rather than like personified abstractions and because these personifications are almost the only characters in the story. For these reasons, the *Psychomachia* had a profound influence on medieval thinking; for a thousand years it stood as the model of the epic struggle between good and evil.[22]

The battle became one of the two major forms that allegorical plots have taken (the other is the journey, quest, or pilgrimage), and we find a similar battle in the *Rose* between the forces of Good (the God of Love and his followers) and Evil (Jealousy, Chastity, and friends). Both works describe a series of hand-to-hand combats between vices and virtues: in the *Psychomachia,* Pudicita against Sodomita Libido, Patientia against Ira, Sobrietas against Luxuria, etc. In these struggles the personifications behave in typical ways—Patientia stays calm while Ira (Anger) becomes so enraged that she kills herself. Though the contexts of the battles are different in the *Rose* and the *Psychomachia* (one moral and theological, the other amorous), the rhetorical procedures are similar. However, Jean is not simply imitating Prudentius's famous work; we will see later how he used the gravity of his model to undercut his presentation of love.

The *Psychomachia* introduces an enormous number of characters in the course of the war, some of which suggest characters in the *Rose*. For example, Pudor (Modesty), a virtue in the Latin work, may be related to the personification of Shame, an evil in the French one. Most of the personifications are simple and static, but some, more dynamic, change and develop. Several vices even impersonate virtues—as do Jean de Meun's False Seeming and Forced Abstinence. Thus, Cupiditas disguises herself as Frugi (Temperance) and tries to tempt the priests. The satiric potential of this character is recognized and exploited in the second part of the *Rose*. However, Amor does not interest Prudentius— he places him among the followers of Luxuria (soft living), along with gluttony and gaming.

Medieval commentators on Prudentius attempted to understand the process of personification whereby an "accident," an invisible quality, can be portrayed as acting like an independent entity. Literary theoreticians of the period agreed that an author was required to create a visible being (Dante speaks of love as an "accidente in sustanzia" in the *Vita nuova,* section 25), in order to represent a quality, which is invisible. It was largely due to his success in representing invisible or abstract qualities that Prudentius was so greatly admired.[23]

The second major allegorical work from late antiquity is Martianus Capella's *De nuptiis Philologiae et Mercurii* (The marriage of Philology and Mercury). The nine books of this long work describe the seven liberal arts in the context of an allegorical wedding between Mercury (Eloquence) and Philology (Love of Learning). The *De nuptiis* became a basic school text in the ninth century and was widely read and commented through the Renaissance (we have almost as many manuscripts of the *De nuptiis* as of the *Rose*). In modern times, however, it has been largely ignored or unappreciated—see C. S. Lewis's discussion in which he refers to "the curiosity shop" of Capella's mind.[24] More recently, scholars have tried to understand the reasons for the work's enormous popularity in the Middle Ages. Winthrop Wetherbee, for example, argues that "it was Martianus' qualities of style and imagination at least as much as his didactic uses which interested the twelfth century."[25]

The first two books of the *De nuptiis* take us on a long allegorical quest to find a bride for Mercury, who is first refused by Sophia (Wisdom, already married to Eternity), Mantice (Prophecy, linked with Apollo), and Psyche (the soul, promised to Cupid). Virtue leads Mercury in search of Apollo, who may be able to suggest a bride. On consulting Apollo, Mercury is told that the wife for him is Philology, who has almost divine insight into the nature of things. But before Mercury can approach Philology, he must obtain the consent of Jupiter, and so he and Virtue set out again, this time accompanied by Apollo and the Muses. When Jupiter and Juno cannot reach a decision, Pallas, divine wisdom, is consulted: she would rather that Philology remain a virgin, like her, but she gives her consent if Philology is first made immortal. The gods are assembled and described in a long catalog; Jupiter and Juno appear at the council dressed in robes representing the visible world and the phenomena of the atmosphere and upper air. The action stops while the allegorical garments are described at length. Finally the gods decide unanimously to immortalize Philology.

Book 2 describes the initiation procedures by which Philology becomes immortal. After she consults the stars and the auspices, which tell her that all bodes well for the marriage, her mother, Phronesis (prudence, understanding) dresses her, and the Muses sing in her honor. The Cardinal Virtues, Philosophy, the Graces, and Athanasia (immortality) arrive and begin the ceremony. First Philology is made to vomit up all the books she has in her and then she drinks a certain "spherical and animate rotundity" that makes her immortal. Finally, ascending to the heavens, passing by the throne of the Sun, and arriving at the Empyrean, Philology beholds the sphere that moves the universe. Juno accompanies the bride, explaining as they go the various demons and spirits that people the air. After Philology prays, kneeling at the outermost limit of the universe, she feels herself, now immortal, ready to approach Jupiter. The marriage decree is read, and Mercury presents his wedding gift—seven wise virgins representing the Seven Liberal Arts.[26]

This brief sketch of a complex poem suggests some of the ways that the *De nuptiis* influenced medieval allegorical thinking. The maturing experiences of a man on a quest, the integration of cosmology and mythology, and the richly ambivalent opportunities for allegorical interpretation, appealed to the learned writers of the twelfth century, who renewed the tradition of the allegorical poem. According to Wetherbee, the *De nuptiis* "dramatizes the theme of intellectual pilgrimage from the sensible world to the level of vision and theology," a theme which the Middle Ages will regard as "virtually the archetypal theme of all serious poetry."[27] The Lover of the Rose goes on a similar pilgrimage, during which he is given the opportunity to mature emotionally and intellectually, though the seriousness with which Jean, unlike Capella, treats this quest is offset with humor to show some of the conflicting positions that can be taken on the object of the quest.

The third work from late antiquity that served as a model for the *Rose* was the *De consolatione philosophiae* (*The Consolation of Philosophy*) of Boethius (ca. 480–524), the most influential late classical work in the Middle Ages and the one most often translated. Even Jean de Meun translated it, after pointing out in the *Rose* that a translation of Boethius's work would do people a lot of good (ll. 5007–10) and translations into English were made by Chaucer, King Alfred the Great, and Queen Elizabeth I. A modern translator, V. E. Watts, claims that "*The Divine Comedy* as a whole can be regarded as a great elaboration" of Boethius's concept of the ascent of the soul and its return to its true home.[28] So important was the work of this late Christian writer for the twelfth century that it has been called the Age of Boethius (but also the Age of Ovid—these two writers, who appear to be totally opposed, shaped much of medieval thought).

Boethius came from an important Latin family, the Anicii, whose members included many consuls, two emperors, and a pope. As a child he showed great interest in and aptitude for study and as a young man was made consul in 510. While in public office he continued his studies; he translated Aristotle's works on logic and wrote five small works of theology, treatises on arithmetic, geometry, music (this treatise remained a textbook at Oxford until the eighteenth century), and perhaps works on astronomy and mechanics. But his last, and greatest, work is *The Consolation of Philosophy,* which he wrote in prison, after being accused (falsely, he claims) of conspiring against King Theodoric.

In passages of prose alternating with verse, the author tells how, when he was lamenting his fate, Philosophy came to speak with him. Gently but firmly she shows him the way back to his true home, back to God and self-knowledge. This education, or ascent, of the soul reflects Platonic and Neoplatonic concepts. The idea of recollection, for example, underlies book 3. Scholars have not agreed on the possible Christian elements of the work, which makes no specific reference to Christian doctrine, but Boethius's thinking agrees in general with Christian beliefs about the attributes of God, the nature of man's free will, and the limits of human understanding.

The Consolation of Philosophy may be considered minimally allegorical, for one of its two characters, Philosophy, is the personification of an abstraction. (This topic will be discussed in more detail in the next chapter.) In any case, whether or not Boethius's *Consolation of Philosophy* is true allegory, we discuss it here because its influence on the *Rose* was so great: it shaped Jean's conception of Lady Reason and her relation to the Lover. Jean also based two important passages on it, Reason's discussion of Fortune (see, for example, ll. 4807–4944) and Nature's long monologue on the question of free will versus divine prescience.

These borrowings are not literal translations but free reworkings of Boethius's ideas, with additional ideas borrowed from Suetonius, John of Salisbury, Seneca, and many others. (Langlois, in his study of the sources of the *Roman de la rose,* lists thirty-six classical and medieval authors in addition to Boethius.) Such a list is only a beginning, however, for we still need a careful analysis of how Jean adapted these authorities to his own point of view. Although working from traditional antecedents, the *Rose* is a personal creation.[29]

After Boethius the author to whom Jean de Meun owes the most is the twelfth-century Latin poet, Alain de Lille (Alanus de Insulis [ca. 1116–ca. 1202]). We know little for certain about him, but his many surviving writings show him to have been a widely read philosopher and theologian. The work to which the *Roman de la rose* is a reply is the *De planctu naturae (The Plaint of Nature)*, written about 1160.[30]

Like Boethius's *Consolation of Philosophy*, Alain's allegory is a dialogue in alternating sections of verse and prose (called Mineppean satire) between the poet and the personification of an abstract idea, Lady Nature. The poet begins with a lamentation on the sinfulness of men, especially the sexual perversions that have become common—homosexual men are described as shamelessly twisting the rules of grammar and logic in their relations with other men. Suddenly Lady Nature appears to the poet, who is in a dreamlike state, for she too is grieved by man's wickedness and wishes to discuss the problem with the poet. After a long description of Nature's allegorical appearance (all the universe is portrayed in her crown and dress), the poet tells how he falls into a swoon at her approach because he does not recognize her. Nature brings him to his senses, identifies herself, and the discussion begins. All creation obeys Nature and God, except man, who, besides pursuing all the vices, will not carry out his procreative role. But why, asks Alain, is man blamed for the sexual perversions that the gods do all the time? Nature warns him not to believe what the poets tell us— poetry is an outer shell of falsehood which ideally contains "the sweeter kernel of truth hidden within."[31]

To explain man's wickedness, Nature recounts the history of the world from her point of view: how God appointed her his vice-regent, to see to it that life continues; how she appointed Venus as her sub-delegate; how Venus betrayed her trust and how all sorts of perversions were created by her illegitimate son, Jocus (Sport). Then, at the poet's urging, Nature condemns at length the other vices that man pursues— Gluttony, Drunkenness, Avarice, Pride, Envy, and Flattery. After Nature has given the poet advice for avoiding these vices, another allegorical figure appears, Hymenaeus (Venus's betrayed husband), who represents marital fidelity. He is followed by four beautiful, chaste young women representing the virtues of chastity, temperance, generosity, and humility, all of whom are saddened by man's sinfulness. Nature decides to act. She sends for Genius, her priest, who properly excommunicates the sinners who engage in irregular sex and all the other vices. And the poet awakens from his "dream and ecstasy and the previous vision of the mystic apparition."[32]

Although the importance of *The Plaint of Nature* for the second part of the *Roman de la rose* was recognized very early, only recently have scholars begun to look carefully at Jean de Meun's adaptation of the earlier work. At first scholars saw Jean as simply lifting material from *The Plaint of Nature*. Ernest Langlois claimed that Jean reread the work when he was writing the *Rose* and noted sections which he could add to his own. Therefore, more than 5,000 verses of the *Rose,* according to Langlois, were "traduits, imités ou inspirés" from *The Plaint of Nature.*[33]

Clearly Jean has incorporated both major ideas and details from the earlier work: the characters of Nature and Genius and their roles in the last movement of the work mirror Alain's characters; Natura's oxymoronic definition of love is adapted and offered by Reason. But the *Rose* changes the meaning and the spirit of these borrowed materials so profoundly that Jean's part of the work can be seen as an overturning of Alain's ideas. To date the best effort to understand Jean's position regarding *The Plaint of Nature* is the study by Winthrop Wetherbee.[34] Jean incorporates some of Natura's characteristics into Reason, but he inverts her relationship with the narrator. This inversion is hinted at by a seemingly minor change in the model: in *The Plaint of Nature,* Natura refuses to use vulgar language to express her thoughts, while Jean's Reason makes a point of calling things by their vulgar names. The Lover "is incapable of heeding Raison and seeking in the *integumanz aus poetes* the meaning of the myth of Saturn," and he rejects her[35] (the *integumanz aus poetes* is the "envelope" or "shell" with which poets cover the kernel of truth).

Jean moves away from *The Plaint of Nature* at the end of Reason's speech, but he rejoins it again with the appearance of Nature 8,500 lines later. Now he can develop more fully his "reply" to Alain. One of the ways he does this is through "a devasting [*sic*] elaboration on Alain's critique of the Chartrian faith in Nature as source and standard of moral law."[36] The ideal cooperation of Nature and Reason has become impossible, and the "face of Nature" is shown by Jean to be largely the product of human artifice and perversion. Finally, Jean radically changes Genius's exhortation by making him preach not virtuous love but exuberant procreation. Genius's sermon is one of the keys to understanding the romance, and we will return to it again later (chapter 3).

In addition to these works by Prudentius, Martianus Capella, Boethius, and Alain de Lille, a number of other allegorical poems from the twelfth and thirteenth centuries may have contributed to the *Rose*'s allegory. Alain de Lille was the author of a second important allegorical work, the *Anticlaudianus* (Against Claudian), a work that refutes Claudian's *Anti Rufinum* (Against Rufinus), a description of a diabolical man. Nature, once again the central character, brings together the Virtues in order to create a new, perfect, man. Prudentia receives the soul from God, Nature fashions the body, and Concordia unites them. The Vices attack this wonderful creation, and a psychomachia ensues in which the Virtues triumph. Love reigns and the Golden Age returns.

Jean's *Rose* shows specific evidence of the influence of the *Anticlaudianus*, for it is in the *Anticlaudianus* that the human individual becomes more than an observer of the struggle, that he takes an active role and becomes one of the protagonists. Alain de Lille's allegory may also have influenced Jean de Meun through the importance that the earlier poet assigns to Venus. In *The Plaint of Nature* her importance was indicated by her position as Nature's *subvicaria,* deputy; in the *Anticlaudianus* Venus becomes an active character: at the head of the horde of vices, she throws her torch into the enemy ranks. Alain presents her as more dangerous than the other vices—so powerful that the hero can only defeat her by first fleeing and then shooting her in the back! Finally, we know that it was from the *Anticlaudianus* that Jean took his description of the House of Fortune (see ll. 5891–6088).

Finally, Jean may have been familiar with another important allegorical work of the twelfth century, the *De universitate mundi* or *Cosmographia* (written about 1150) of Bernard Silvestris. The *De universitate* is one of the first works of the twelfth century to incorporate personified abstractions and one of the works that influenced Alain de Lille's conception of allegory. It explains the creation of the world using the model of Plato's *Timaeus* (the only work of Plato's known at that time) and its commentaries. *Noys* (the divine mind) and *Natura* (again) are the principal agents of this creation. The world is described, from the angels and the stars to the earth, its animals, rivers, and medicinal plants. (This poetic desire to encompass creation can be seen again in Nature's robes in *The Plaint of Nature* and in Nature's speech in the *Rose*; it can also be seen in the encyclopedic writers of this period.) Nature then decides to create the "microcosm," that is, man. An allegorical journey ensues that takes Nature to the Supreme Good, then to Venus and Cupid, and finally to Physis (the force that structures matter) and her daughters, Theory and Practice. Together they fashion man on the model of the universe. The description of their creation ends with a celebration of the male sexual organs, which, Bernard says, are not only agreeable to use but which combat death and restore Nature.[37]

Scholars have debated the relative importance of the pagan and Christian elements in this work without finding agreement.[38] It is clear, however, that Jean's views of nature and of the procreative function of man were shaped by works such as the *De universitate* and others from the Chartrian poets of the twelfth century.

In addition to these Latin works, a series of allegories in French preceded the *Roman de la rose*. In fact, Hans Robert Jauss has argued that the latter work cannot be explained simply by the Latin allegories of the twelfth century.[39] Between 1180 and 1220, Christian authors began to write their interpretations of the Bible in French, thus putting them within the reach of any literate person. These works are part of a tradition of exegesis (the finding of meaning in a work, especially the Scriptures) that used allegory to interpret biblical stories, which were seen as having a *sensus literalis* (the narrative itself) and a second, moral or theological, meaning. For example, the story of the taking of Jerusalem by the king of Babylon (2 Kings 25) was glossed as the soul tempted (besieged) by Satan;[40] this example was frequently used in the schools as a model of allegorical exegesis.

When Christian writers wanted to save their beloved Greek and Latin authors from condemnation by the church, they attempted to allegorize them (to give a Christian interpretation to seemingly heretical stories). Almost all classical authors were "moralized" in this way, but Ovid was the one most clearly in need of saving through reinterpretation. The result, the *Ovide moralisé,* became one of the most popular works of the Middle Ages. The *Rose* itself was "allegorized" in the late Middle Ages, and again by some scholars in the twentieth century (see below, chapter 5).

An allegorical poet may work from either end of the composite creation that is allegory, that is, either by taking a preexisting story (the literal meaning) to which the poet gives a second, allegorical, level of meaning, or by creating a story to express certain given truths. Thus the exegetical writer gives an allegorical interpretation to a biblical text, whereas Bernard Sylvestris and Alain de Lille created their own text to which the reader gives an allegorical interpretation (usually with the help of the author). But both kinds of works resulted from the desire to use allegory to express profound truths about the nature of the universe. By creating poetry that expressed such truths, the allegorical poets were saving poetry from the charge, common until the Renaissance, that the stories it told were frivolous, devoid of substance. The early allegorical poets writing in French frequently protest that their religious poems differ from "fables" like the romances of the period, which are "mensonges" (lies). Guillaume de Lorris was the first non-Latin poet to insist that a work that is clearly a fictional creation also has this higher allegorical truth.

The allegorical works in French that appeared between 1180 and the *Roman de la rose* show a clear evolution toward the complex allegorical elements of the *Rose* (Jauss discusses seventeen works).[41] The earliest works consist of simple biblical exegeses based on procedures developed in homiletic writing. One of these, a paraphrase of the *Song of Songs*, shows the growing importance of personifications, for it is they who interpret the meaning of the story, rather than the author (as was customary).

A new stage was reached in the first quarter of the thirteenth century when Raoul de Houdenc, in the *Songe d'enfer* (Dream of Hell), took the theme of the voyage to the other world and linked it to the dream and the personification of the vices. Furthermore, he told the story in the first person. Another innovation of this important work was the substitution of a satiric intention for the moral goals of previous allegorical works. His second allegorical work, *Le roman des ailes* (The romance of the wings), used a religious motif for a nonreligious purpose, to express the true meaning of knighthood.

Le dit des quatre soeurs appears to be the first work in French that delays the allegorical explanation of the story, thus creating a poetic effect of tension and ambivalence. Most allegorical works between 1220 and 1230 adopt this procedure, including the *Roman de la rose,* whose authors promise to give us the allegorical meaning of the work at the end.

Two important works that were probably contemporary with the first part of the *Rose* are *Le roman de miserere* (ca. 1229) of Du Renclus de Moiliens and *Le tournoiement de l'antechrist* (The Tournament of the Antichrist [ca. 1234]) of Huon de Méry. The first shows so many similarities with the *Rose* that it is tempting to see it as an immediate predecessor (as Jauss appears to do), but since the dates of both works are uncertain we cannot be sure which influenced the other. We find in the *Miserere,* for example, courtly vocabulary used to express the relationship of man to God, a beautiful garden surrounded by a high wall, the soul compared to a house with four guards, and characters like Fear, Slander, and Idleness. The author also develops a long allegory of the rose as a symbol of martyred virgins (an image surprisingly appropriate to Jean de Meun's description of the rape of the Rose).

The Tournament of the Antichrist is an imaginative work in the tradition of Prudentius's *Psychomachia* but one that offers few similarities with the *Rose*. When the author went to the forest of Broceliande to test the magic fountain (the same one that appears in Chrétien de Troyes's *Yvain*), he unleashed a horde of vices led by the Prince of Hell. The Antichrist joins them to fight in a tournament against the forces of Heaven—among whom we find King Arthur and his best knights! Although the poet sometimes speaks in his own voice, of his own experiences, he cannot introduce his persona into the central part of the action except as a chronicler.

Thus most of the allegorical ideas and images found in the *Rose* were to be found in earlier literary works. But several crucial steps remained to be taken by Guillaume de Lorris in order to realize the potential of extended allegory: the use of allegory to express a vision of love; the union of two levels of meaning, the general and the particular, that of Man and of a particular man; and the use of the dream vision for a frame that legitimates the story.

Dream Visions

Dreams have appeared in literature for almost as long as people have wondered about their meaning. Classical philosophers, such as Galen, Aristotle, Artemidorus, and Plotinus, tried to explain dreams and classify them according to their causes, while writers, such as Homer, Aeschylus (in *The Persians*), and Cicero, recounted dreams in their literary works. The Middle Ages continued this long tradition of explaining and interpreting dreams and of using them as a literary framework. In addition to the works of classical authors, the Bible offered the Middle Ages examples of dreams, "true" (prophetic) ones this time, so medieval thinkers could not treat all dreams as natural phenomena. The difficulty was in distinguishing dreams sent by divine or diabolic forces from those caused by physiological or psychological processes. Popular handbooks with keys to interpreting dreams circulated in the Middle Age, often to the disapproval of the church, and both philosophers and theologians tried to find a way to distinguish prophetic dreams from fantasies.

In the Middle Ages, the most famous literary dream of late antiquity was the *Somnium Scipionis* (The dream of Scipio) with which Cicero ends his *De republica*. This dream was known primarily through a commentary on it by Macrobius (ca. 400) that became a basic text in medieval culture (there are numerous references to it in Chaucer's works, for example). A modern translator has explained the work's importance in this way: "Perhaps no other book of comparably small size contained so many subjects of interest and doctrines that are repeatedly found in medieval literature."[42] In addition to a classification of dreams, Macrobius discusses the nature of poetry and myth, a classification of the virtues, how man differs from animals and plants, and the proof that the earth is in the center of the universe.

This is the authority to whom Guillaume refers as "un auctor qui ot non Macrobes, / qui ne tint pas songes a lobes" (ll. 7–8; an author named Macrobius, who did not think all dreams were false). Guillaume does not refer specifically to Macrobius's five-part classification of dreams but uses the Latin author's reputation for expertise to support his assertion that his dream about the God of Love was indeed prophetic. Guillaume's *Rose* is evidently the first time that a dream became the vehicle for amorous (as opposed to didactic) literature. Later even serious didactic poets turned to the *Rose* and its successors for their allegories.[43]

Why does Guillaume choose to tell his allegory of love as though it were a dream? He tells us that the God of Love ordered him to tell this dream (l. 33), thus suggesting that the dream was a message from the divinity himself. In this way Guillaume gives the romance an air of truth, of authenticity, that a fictional narrative would not have. As Hieatt expresses it, "The dream convention lends a certain sort of authority, and authority was dear to the medieval public."[44] In addition, the dream setting is an appropriate vehicle for the type of allegory that Guillaume is creating—the personified abstractions, the sudden and surprising reversals, the unreal atmosphere of much of the setting—all these elements are more believable in the context of a dream. Finally, it may be the dream pretext that allows Guillaume to tell the story in the first person (no romance before the *Rose* does so), for he is telling us his dream in which he was the protagonist. Thus the dream form allows Guillaume to play with the tension that arises between the many roles the poet plays in the narration: dreamer, narrator, lover.[45]

Jean de Meun, as a student of Aristotle, shows himself to be skeptical of the truth of dreams, which he has Nature discuss as an afterthought to her summary of optical illusions. Nature reviews the reason for believing that all dreams have natural explanations; as for those that may be sent by God or devils, she refrains from comment (ll. 18274–484). And the second part of the *Rose* is less dreamlike than the first; it is much less visual and much more realistic, through the interventions of such characters as False Seeming and the Old Woman. For Jean does not present his poem as a transcription of his own experience; he is not the dreamer—or the lover.

All the elements of the medieval dream vision (the dream that tells a love story) are in place in Guillaume's romance, and they will be used by many poets over the next three centuries, as we will see in chapter 4.

Intellectual Influences

During a discussion of Jean de Meun's debt to Aristotle, one scholar argued that Aristotelianism, even in the thirteenth century, held little importance in Christian thought, while another asserted that Jean de Meun's theory was clearly Averroïstic.[46] This exchange between two eminent medievalists over the importance of Aristotelian thought in Jean de Meun's work shows the difficulties that scholars have encountered when they have tried to characterize the philosophical orientation of the second part of the *Rose*. The problem results from the complexity of medieval Scholasticism, which was a monumental attempt to understand, classify, and evaluate classical philosophical thinking, and which was therefore an interweaving of Platonic, Neoplatonic, and, from the thirteenth century on, Aristotelian ideas, as they came through Arab and Jewish translators and interpreters, such as Avicenna (980–1037), Averroës (1126–98), and Maimonides (1135–1204).[47]

Since Jean de Meun's work reflects the complex intellectual milieu of the third quarter of the thirteenth century, a time of great intellectual turbulence, evidence for both Platonic and Aristotelian concepts can be—and have been—pointed to by scholars. Two extreme positions are represented by Ernest Langlois's assertion that "Jean de Meun n'a pas fait grand usage des écrits d'Aristote: il ne les cite que trois fois" (Jean de Meun did not make much use of Aristotle's writings) and Gérard Paré's contention that "L'inspiration foncière du roman de Jean de Meun remonte à l'aristotélisme universitaire du 13ᵉ siècle" (The fundamental inspiration for Jean de Meun's romance goes back to thirteenth-century university Aristotelianism).[48] Paré and others point to the prevalence in the *Rose* of Scholastic terminology relating to rhetoric and logic, to the critical practices used in the schools, and to certain Aristotelian principles of natural science.

Unfortunately, most attempts to situate Jean de Meun's "philosophy" have oversimplified this difficult problem, either by equating Scholasticism with Aristotelianism (which is inaccurate) or by arguing that Jean alludes to Averroïstic (Aristotelian) theses, without evaluating Jean's attitude toward them. Thus it is not helpful to say that Jean "directly touches upon" the Averroïstic position of the denial of divine providence[49] without pointing out that Jean rejects that position, and that he does so by using Boethius's largely Platonic arguments. The analysis that gives the most careful appraisal of Jean's Platonic Aristotelianism is Lucie Polak's "Plato, Nature and Jean de Meun." Her complex argument can perhaps be summarized as saying that Jean's Nature is "an enthusiastically Aristotelian Nature" who is used by the author to explode Alain de Lille's Platonic Nature and who is in turn destroyed by Genius, who reduces her message to that of some of the heterodox propositions condemned by the church in 1277.

This difficult problem is not simply a question of literary history, although more careful study of the intellectual milieu at the time of the *Rose* will help us to understand the problem. It is also the pivot on which an understanding of the second part of the *Rose* rests, and so we will return to it again in the last chapter.

Another problematic aspect of Jean's work, one that also concerns the nature of the Scholastic endeavor, is the question of whether Jean was writing an encyclopedic work. Although some comprehensive works had been written in antiquity, such as Pliny's *Historia naturalis,* it was in the thirteenth century that Western authors began to classify all that was known at the time. About 1260 Vincent de Beauvais began his monumental *Speculum majus* (Great mirror), probably the greatest encyclopedia before the eighteenth century (a century with which the thirteenth shares many similarities). Its three parts covered human history from the Creation up to Louis IX, summarized all known natural history and scientific knowledge, and provided a thorough compendium on literature, law, politics, and economics. It was influential, especially on Chaucer, and was still respected in the Italian Renaissance. Other important encyclopedic works from the thirteenth century are Brunetto Latini's *Le trésor* (written in French) and St. Thomas Aquinas's *Summa theologiae*. These colossal works point to a desire to know everything, and to tell all ("car il fet bon de tout savoir," writes Jean in the *Rose,* 1. 15184; for it's good to know everything).

Do Nature's discussions in the *Rose* on optics, the effects of the heavenly bodies on human beings, and other such topics constitute digressions from the subject of the work? That is, is Jean simply giving in to the urge to tell his public everything that he knows, as though he were writing an encyclopedia? Early scholars of the *Rose*, not knowing what to think of this seemingly unconnected material, simply dismissed it as "an encyclopedia" (Gérard Paré: "la seconde partie du Roman de la Rose est à la fois un roman et une encyclopédie" [The second part of the *Romance of the rose* is at once a romance and an encyclopedia]). The opposite point of view is represented by Alan Gunn, who has argued that everything in the work (or almost everything) has its reason for being there, and that the *Rose* is an artistic whole.[50]

I agree with Gunn that Jean is using discussions that appear to us digressive for literary purposes—to characterize, to criticize, to elaborate a theme that is important to him. Jean's part of the *Rose* is closer to the kind of work called a "miroir," which developed various aspects of a subject for didactic purposes—to teach noblemen to be better noblemen, or lovers, better lovers (see l. 10621, "li Miroer aus Amoreus," the mirror for lovers). Thus, it is no longer adequate to dismiss one or another part of the *Rose* as simply the encyclopedic urge of a Scholastic writer. Most scholars now try to understand the literary motives behind even the scientific discussions.

The *Roman de la rose* has been described as the synthesis of medieval culture in the thirteenth century. We have looked briefly at all the major traditions flowing into this remarkable synthesis; we can now look more closely at the way the *Rose* adapts these traditions in its varied use of allegory and in its major personifications: Reason, Nature, and Genius.

Chapter Three
Allegory and Personification in the *Rose*

The *Roman de la rose,* the greatest allegorical poem in French, is frequently studied for the variety of allegorical techniques that the authors used. Guillaume de Lorris created an allegorical world that expressed, in a courtly setting, the psychological and social processes that occur when a person loves or is loved. Jean de Meun was more interested in the philosophical potential of the various personifications of authority which the allegorical form offered. In this chapter we will discuss the allegorical techniques of the two parts of the *Rose* and the major personifications, Reason, Nature, and Genius.

Allegory in the *Rose*

"Allegory" is one of the oldest critical terms, yet there is still little agreement among scholars as to what it means.[1] It has been defined as a way of reading or a way of writing, as very broad (the process of interpretation itself) or very narrow (simply personification), as a vehicle for truth or an obsolete fancy. And whenever it has been discussed, at least since the Renaissance, it has nearly always been viewed negatively. Carolynn Van Dyke has summarized (perhaps tongue-in-cheek) the critical history of allegory as that of the Other: "allegory has always functioned among literary kinds as the Other"[2]. That is, allegory is either set against a literary form that is positively valued (symbolism, or realism, for example), or it is declared to have no meaning at all. Arnold Williams, for example, rejects the term: "I have found 'allegorical' a splendid term to cover up one's ignorance, but a useless one for communicating any valuable information."[3] Yet the *Roman de la rose* is believed to be an excellent example of an allegory, so we must try to understand the concept in relation to this work.

The standard definition of "allegory," at least until recently, was "saying one thing and meaning another" (the Greek *allos* means

"other," so otherness is incorporated into the etymology of allegory).
Thus Quintillian, first century Roman rhetorician: "Allegory . . .
either presents one thing in words and another in meaning, or else
something absolutely opposed to the meaning of the words."[4] Many
scholars since the first century have repeated the "two-level" theory of
allegory, that there is a skin or shell of story covering a kernel of truth.
At bottom this approach does not get us very far, for many literary
(and some nonliterary) modes "say X and mean Y," such as irony, symbol, myth, icon, advertising slogans, even speech itself, according to
modern linguistic theories that stress the disjunction of the signifier
and the signified. Allegory in this sense is "the interpretative process
itself."[5]

Allegories like the *Roman de la rose* (works written as allegories, in
distinction to works upon which later allegorical interpretations are
imposed) appear to indicate that figurative levels of significance are
intended by the work itself. Indications may or may not be given as to
the nature of the other meanings, but we know that they are supposed
to be there. In this way allegory differs from modes such as irony,
which incorporates several points of view concerning one level of meaning. Thus, allegory often suggests a more abstract meaning behind the
more concrete surface meaning; or, as Van Dyke has expressed it, allegory is "a shift of perspective to include both concrete agents and the
intelligible realities in which they participate."[6]

Problems have developed when scholars have viewed this synthesis
as incorporating two distinct but consistently parallel levels. Either the
literal level is devalued in order to see the figurative meaning as the
essential one, or the figurative level is seen as tacked on to a good story
to give it a veneer of morality or doctrine. Those who follow the first
path argue that once we have extracted the allegorical meaning, we
have "read" the work. This view of allegory has led scholars to see it
as contrived, a mode of expression rather than a mode of thought.[7]
When such readings have failed to find neat parallels between the two
levels, scholars have blamed the allegorical work for not following the
formula that they imposed on it.[8]

Several important works on allegory have argued against reading it
in this way: "proper allegorical ambiguity" in a work like the *Rose*
requires that we give equal attention to the so-called "literal" and the
figurative levels of the work, and that we leave the reading open to
figurative meanings on a number of levels.[9] The usefulness of this understanding of allegory is shown by the fact that it removes the con-

fusion created by attempts to precisely delineate the referent for an allegorical character like Jealousy (the lady's husband? parents? guardian? her own feelings?) or the Rose (the beloved? her love? her beauty? her ultimate favor? her pudenda?)[10]

Some scholars have perceptively described the levels on which Guillaume's allegory functions, the way characters move from the lyric to the narrative to the didactic mode, the way an idea is expressed both in a character and in an object. Jean-Charles Payen, who carried out such an analysis, argues that "the author invents his figures of speech as narration requires them, without worrying about the internal coherence or rigor of his work."[11] He sees in Guillaume's allegory "a series of semiological ruptures," "several discordant semiological systems," and concludes that Guillaume may not have had a plan for what he was doing. But we often find in medieval allegory surprising eruptions of characters who do not "fit" according to our conception of coherence or rigor (the arrival of King Arthur and his knights in the *Tournament of the Antichrist,* for example). In this way medieval allegory is like modern fantasy or science fiction literature, in which the reader is taken to a strange, wonderful land where things are not what they seem at first, where anything can happen, and where the experience unfolds slowly to reveal its meaning only at the end (if at all).

It is not simply that the figurative meaning of an allegorical element may shift throughout the story, as the point of view of the speakers shifts, but that an allegorical reading that respects the text sees constantly both the particular beloved and the Beloved—an abstract level that was more real, in medieval thinking, than the concrete. This is Van Dyke's fundamental view of allegory, the narrative of universals, that it "envisions human life as a continual interchange between temporal event and eternal pattern."[12]

In addition to this fundamental problem of the levels of allegory, many other questions have arisen from the complex nature of the mode: the distinction between allegory as a mode of reading and allegory as a mode of writing, or between allegory and symbolism; whether a literary frame, such as romance, is necessary; how to read the subspecies called "personification allegory" (or whether it is allegory at all).[13] The most helpful hypotheses have often come from scholars who have analysed individual texts closely. And fortunately for our purposes, the *Rose* is one of the medieval texts that is often scrutinized. Since I cannot consider here the allegory of the *Rose* in great detail, the following discussion will focus on the larger narrative patterns that have been suggested, the principal theories of the significance of the allegorical narrative, and the poetic elements by which the allegory is expressed, especially in the first part.

W. T. H. Jackson has argued that allegorical narrative is not an independent form, that personifications must be placed in a literary context with which the audience is familiar: "Only by giving [abstractions] a milieu outside everyday life but within the experience of the reader can they be made real."[14] Thus, the Vergilian epic was the frame for the *Psychomachia,* the marriage feast of the gods for the *Marriage of Mercury and Philology,* the courtly romance for the *Roman de la rose.*[15] More precisely, the Lover in the *Rose* sets out in a world that is a mixture of lyric and romance motifs, but he ends in a situation, according to Jackson, that corresponds to "the conclusion of what is normally the first part of a romance."[16]

Which of these frames a reader chooses for the allegory of the *Rose* has consequences for the interpretation of the ending, that is, for our view of whether the work is unfinished (suggested by a romance framework) or finished (the last section resembles the end of many courtly lyrics).[17] Furthermore, one of the reasons that readers may often see the second part as digressive, disjointed, and disunified, is that Jean de Meun does not stay with one or two major frames but moves from Platonic dialogue to fabliau to satiric monologue to epic to cosmology to homelitic and back to fabliau (among others).

Other larger narrative patterns that have been suggested for the first part of the *Rose* include the bildungsroman (the education of a young man), the initiation rite, and the so-called "visionary landscape." The first two patterns are closely related to the structure of romance, which usually takes the form of a young man's quest that leads him to a new identity. The visionary landscape, one of the forms that classical and medieval personification allegories have often taken, is examined by Paul Piehler.[18] In Boethius's *Psychomachia,* Alain de Lille's *The Plaint of Nature,* and in both parts of the *Rose,* a recurring pattern occurs in which a dreamer is "profoundly disturbed by some spiritual crisis; he has a vision of mysterious import which is interpreted by persons in spiritual authority, and the effect of the vision and its interpretation is to resolve the crisis, often by raising him to a higher spiritual state."[19] Used in a restrained and ambivalent way in the first part, this pattern explodes in the second part to give us Jean's most subtle allegorical writing.

Visionary allegory is a manifestation of one of the earliest functions of the mode, the concealment of higher mysteries of which the uninitiated can be given only quick glimpses, if at all. In the *Rose* both authors promise several times to reveal the deeper meaning of their words, but both seem to defer until it is too late (for example, 1. 1600: "quant j'avré apost le mistère," when I will have explained the mystery). When we look for the hidden truth in the words of their "figures of authority," however, the veil of mystery remains intact.

At the beginning of the *Rose* there is no indication of a crisis brewing in the dream life of the Lover, for the wonderful garden to which he has been admitted seems to be an earthly paradise. Each step he takes, however, each apparently unconstrained choice he makes, brings him closer to the moment of truth (of a kind). "Guillaume has given subtle expression to the process of succumbing to temptation,"[20] and this temptation—the desire for the Rose—brings on the crisis, the traumatic event of falling in love, represented by the piercing arrows of the God of Love. Here is the first *potentia*, or figure of authority, who will respond to the poor Lover's anguish by explaining the mysterious laws of love to him. But Guillaume's ambivalent view of this "authority" is indicated by the fact that it is this very divinity who has caused the crisis.

Guillaume's next authority, the Friend, reassures the dreamer a little and gives him some practical advice, but the consequences of following this advice are disastrous. The last authority, Reason, is rejected by the dreamer after her short speech of remonstrance. Guillaume has multiplied his authorities and set one against another. So although his romance appears to be following the pattern described by Piehler, Guillaume's ambiguous view of authority leads to some original variations on the pattern, variations that may spring from ambivalence in his view of the nature of love itself.

If the speeches of the main characters in Jean de Meun's part were removed, there would remain about 4,000 lines of narrative and dialogue—the same number of lines as Guillaume's part. Thus, Jean's continuation is structured by this succession of authorities (*doctores amoris*, professors of love, in Gunn's terms).[21] These figures of authority are also the focus for most of the criticism written on the allegorical structure of the second part. (We will discuss the major figures of authority in detail in the second part of this chapter.) The way Jean uses these figures is a brilliant realization of allegory's potential, while at the same time, in Rosemund Tuve's words, a "difficult and dangerous method . . . a kind of weaving dance-like movement, a dialectic in which no figure is Auctor . . . ."[22]

The figures of authority—Reason, Friend, False Seeming, the Old Woman, Nature, and Genius—oppose each other in a way that leaves the reader without an authoritative definition of love. What for Piehler is Jean's failure to make a clear statement concerning the hierarchical relationship of his *potentiae* (a failure that the critic attributes to the dreamer's state of mind) is for Rosemund Tuve the result of Jean's "method of sustained irony," in which no one is identified with the right side.[23] Marc-René Jung argues that this conflict of authorities points to the work's meaning: "C'est le jeu dialectique des oppositions qui fait ressortir le sens de l'oeuvre" (It is the dialectic play of the oppositions that brings out the meaning of the work).[24] Our final view of love, therefore, is the result of this complex debate in which the reader must make the final decision.

The reader rather than the Lover, for he does not hear all the speeches (not as actor, only as dreamer). The relation of the authorities to the main character is more complex in the second part of the *Rose* than in other allegorical works built on this pattern (*The Plaint of Nature*, for example). The Lover is the object of the speeches of only two of the six major authorities—Reason and Friend. He hears about the Old Woman's lecture only indirectly, from Warm Welcome himself; Nature's "confession" is given offstage; Genius exhorts the entire army of Love; finally, False Seeming speaks to the God of Love primarily, with the Lover and the barons overhearing. In any case, the Lover has fairly well made up his mind back in the first part, and, with only brief lapses, remains loyal to his first teacher. It is the *Rose*'s audience, therefore, that hears all the arguments and renders judgment in this enormous "question d'amour."

False Seeming differs fundamentally from the other authorities: he does not speak directly about love, he has nothing to gain from aiding the Lover's cause, he appears to be talking simply to reveal himself. This was of course a simple way for Jean to present his satire of the Mendicant Orders and his support for Guillaume de Saint-Amour, one of their principal opponents.[25] This conflict, which had begun in the first third of the century, reached a crisis about 1269 ("In a period from 1269 to 1271, twenty-nine known polemics had been issued by the seculars and the mendicants against each other").[26] The problem was therefore of great interest at the time that Jean was probably writing his continuation.

But what led Jean to include this long speech by False Seeming, representing the Mendicants, in his allegory of love? Was he moved simply by partisan motives? The satire of the Mendicants that is expressed through False Seeming exaggerates their supposed vices in the tradition of medieval anticlerical satire (churchman were the second favorite topic of satire in the Middle Ages, after women). But Jean goes beyond topicality and tradition to develop an amusing but frightening portrait of hypocrisy, of a medieval trickster figure, all the more frightening because False Seeming's intelligence serves his complete immorality.

And yet False Seeming is the only character who simply speaks from his own experience, who is not trying to persuade someone of something, the only character who is frank with us. Or is he? He has constructed his own appearance, a false one; he cannot be known by his membership in a social group, an important way of knowing people in the Middle Ages. And his paradoxical revelations are made by someone who opposes revelation (it is significant that he kills Bad Mouth for speaking the truth, and that he kills him in private confession, the form of truth-speaking urged by the church). False Seeming seems to speak candidly of his own experiences, but can he be trusted? This disturbing ambiguity in the relation of words to experience is one of the fundamental problems that concern Jean (see below, chapter 6).

These complex structural patterns underlying the *Rose*'s allegory of love carry the load of significance that critics have observed in the romance. The hypotheses concerning the figurative meaning of the work, especially of the first part, fall into four major categories. The simplest and most literal takes Guillaume at his word when he says that the dream was prophetic: "en ce songe onques riens n'ot / qui tretot avenu ne soit / si con li songes recensoit" (ll. 28–30; there was nothing in this dream that did not come completely true, just as the dream told it). It is perhaps to lend credence to this assertion that the narrator tells us that five years have passed since the dream—time enough for the events described to have really occurred. We can imagine an audience listening to the *Rose* (medieval works were frequently read aloud) and speculating on the real counterparts to the events and characters of the dream. Although "there is nothing unlikely in the theory that his poem is autobiographical,"[27] the dream events are so general that it is hard to imagine that they cover a unique experience. Therefore, many scholars go beyond the *roman à clé* to the level of a typical psychological experience of love.

C. S. Lewis was the first to develop a coherent interpretation of the first part of the *Rose* as psychological fiction, more specifically, as "a realistic account of imaginative passion," in accord with his theory that the purpose of allegory generally is "to supply the subjective element in literature, to paint the inner world."[28] Consequently his "interpretation" of the story is a retelling that attempts to match a sentimental event to the allegorical events, with more or less success (is Jealousy an aspect of the girl's personality or does it represent her parents?). This approach allows Lewis to proclaim that in the end "we have an intimate knowledge" of the heroine.[29] Although many scholars have accepted this approach, others feel that it is reductive, that in effect it is a modern attempt to allegorize the *Rose*; Tuve, for example, protests that "this substitution of psychological naturalism for metaphorical action is an unfortunate narrowing, influenced by the combined overimportance of the novel and of psychological description. The *Roman de la Rose* is a vastly larger work than any novel could be. . . ."[30]

If the *Rose* is not the medieval equivalent of a psychological case study, it is nonetheless about love, or rather about kinds of love, courtly and other. Guilllaume himself tells us that his work encloses the "whole art of love" (l. 38; "ou l'art d'Amors est tote enclose;" which contains the whole art of love). Many details in the first part indicate that we are not simply watching a young man court a young woman, but that the ideals (or ideology) of courtly (noble) society are being unfolded before us—for example, in the contrast between the repulsive, common types of people painted on the outer wall of the garden and the elegant, graceful dancers inside (one of whom is even named Cortoisie, Courtliness). The Lover has the desire to be part of the angelic couples around Merriment—to accomplish which he need only fall in love (which he promptly manages to do). Furthermore, the God of Love expounds to him the perfect courtly way of life as well as the rules of true love. Finally, the fact that the Lover first sees the image of the roses, rather than real flowers, and that he sees the class (roses) before the individual (this rose), suggests that it is the ideal rather than the reality that attracted the poet.

Is Guillaume naively extolling the courtly illusions of his time or gently mocking them? Most critics who see the work as an allegory of courtly values argue that Guillaume took those values seriously, at least as an ideal: "Le *Roman de la Rose* nous dit comment la cour se rêve" (The *Roman de la rose* tells how the court dreams itself to be).[31] Guillaume appears to believe in an ideal love, set in an ideal society, although the Lover is only dimly aware of a higher meaning to his desire to possess the Rose.

Another theory of the significance of the *Rose* interprets the allegory as a retelling of the Fall from Paradise, an interpretation developed by D. W. Robertson, John R. Fleming, and their students. Fleming expresses it succinctly: "Adam plucks an apple; Amant, the *bouton*."[32] However, despite the quotations from ecclesiastical authorities alleged to support this hypothesis, it has not received wide critical acceptance, in part because too much must be ignored or explained away to make this approach plausible (see the further discussion in chapter 5).

The first part of the *Rose* suggests these larger allegorical structures and figurative meanings through the text's poetic realization, in particular through the use of personification and symbolism. An example of each will illustrate Guillaume's subtle poetic technique.

Many scholars have in effect equated allegory with personification; Maureen Quilligan, for example, defines allegory as "narrative peopled by personified abstractions moving about a reechoing landscape of language.[33] However, it is inaccurate to take personification for allegory as such, according to Douglas Kelly, the author of a major study of medieval literary theory and practice, although he points out that personification is common in allegory, especially in romance in the Middle Ages.[34] Other scholars have argued that personifications are not allegory at all, because they are what they seem, there is no hidden meaning: "Characters are never allegoric. They are literal; they mean what their names say they mean."[35] Thus Frank argues that a personification is allegoric only by its actions and relationships, not by its words.

Yet if this were true—that personifications are simply what their names say they are—readers would not disagree so frequently on the meaning of personifications, even static, apparently simple, ones like Guillaume's images on the wall of the garden. Furthermore, those scholars who have naively taken the words of the *Roman*'s characters at face value have missed their ironic implications, as we shall see in the case of Genius especially.

The *Roman de la rose,* the most developed example of medieval personification allegory, offers a great variety of allegorical abstractions. Douglas Kelly summarizes in this way the three principal types of personifications found in the first part of the *Rose*: "first, the Images painted into the wall of Deduit's garden and illustrating defects that impede courtly love; second, the personifications participating in the song and carol inside the garden and representing qualities essential to the *fin amant*; and third, the personifications, gods, and goddesses appearing in the narrative proper centering on the Rose and depicting the adventures of and changes in the Lover in his pursuit of the Rose."[36] Kelly has shown how Guillaume uses varied rhetorical techniques to guide his readers in their response to these personifications.[37]

Guillaume's first set of abstractions, which differ from true personifications by being static icons, are described in some detail, but the descriptions are not intended to differentiate them, for many of the same ideas are repeated from one defect to the next, from Hate to Felony to Villainy, for example. Guillaume is attempting to convey vituperation of ignoble qualities, rather than realistic portraits, as Chaucer might do. In a similar way, the personifications of noble qualities in the Garden are not analytically described but share similar properties: splendor, light, beauty, and proportion.[38] Guillaume further emphasizes the difference between the noble personification and the ignoble paintings by showing the inhabitants of the Garden in motion, acting out the highest forms of courtly joy—dancing, singing, dallying. As the paintings on the wall repelled the Lover, so the personifications in the Garden strongly attract him by their portrayal of "joy as a predisposition to love."[39]

The apparent simplicity of the images on the wall fades when we attempt to interpret what they mean for our understanding of the garden. Are they meant to show which qualities are not admitted to the Garden? But some of them, such as Old Age, do appear in the Garden (in the Old Woman). We would expect to find portraits of the Seven Deadly Sins on the wall, since they are often portrayed in medieval art and architecture, and this is what the Robertsonians has chosen to do, by leaving aside the three portraits that are not vices.[40] Most simply, however, these portraits indicate the qualities that are not acceptable in a *fin'amant* (courtly lover), as the Lover learns from the God of Love.

Once in the Garden our problems of interpretation increase, beginning with the garden itself, in which a number of symbols have raised discussion. The rich literary, religious, and iconographical history of the *locus amoenus,* the garden of delight, earthly paradise, ideal landscape, would seem to guide our interpretation but instead it complicates it.[41] Is this Heaven on Earth, as the impressionable Lover claims (see especially ll. 637–40), an allegory of the Garden of Eden, as Fleming claims, or "the life of the court"?[42] The answer will reflect the assumption that we are reading a psychological, theological, or sociological work.

But perhaps the most difficult allegory of all is not the garden as a whole but one small part of it, the two crystals in the Fountain of Narcissus that reflect the wonders of the garden, including its rose bushes. Because most manuscripts mention two crystals (representing the two streams that flow into the fountain?), most interpreters opt for either the lady's eyes (or a prefiguration of her eyes, since the rose itself is not reflected in the pool), or the lover's eyes. In a close textual analysis of the passage, Larry H. Hillman attempts to disprove both interpretations. Instead, he argues that "Amant's experiences in the garden have been a series of tests of his character and his receptiveness to the way of life in the garden. . . . His examination of the crystals is the final test. Knowing that his lack of excessive pride will protect him from meeting Narcissus's fate, he avoids his own image and carefully and completely examines the objects revealed by the mirror before going off to select his rosebud . . . the crystals . . . serve as the mechanism by which Amour tests a potential lover's will and ability to choose a suitable love object."[43] This hypothesis, the only one that takes into account all the relevant details in the text, makes the most sense of this mysterious episode.

Yet the mystery remains. Allegory is not meant to be a realistic genre in the nineteenth-century meaning, although realistic details are found in it. It both raises and lowers its subjects; it transposes a higher reality (love), one that cannot be expressed in words, to a more mundane level and shows individual things (the Lover) as part of a class. This quality of great allegory pleases some, who see it as an aspect of all poetry, displeases others, who find such fanciful shells inappropriate for the kernel of truth within.[44]

Chinese boxes may be a better image for Guillaume's polyvalent allegory: a true confession inside a psychological case study inside a hyperbolic portrait of court society inside a reenactment of Adam's Fall. Van Dyke summarizes Guillaume's allegory this way: "Guillaume realizes at least two kinds of complexity always latent in allegory: an equivocation about the ontological status of abstractions and an ambivalence between absolute and contingent values." And the characters seem to know that they live in an ambivalent, invented world—the Lover certainly doesn't act as if he has been shot with arrows, but he goes along with the game.[45] But it is a serious game that drew in readers for centuries after the composition of the *Rose* and still has the power to draw us in today.

Jean de Meun's allegory is as polyvalent as that of Guillaume—to judge by the amount of scholarly disagreement that it has caused. Not only is there disagreement about the figurative meaning of the second part but also about its quality in comparison with Guillaume's subtlety and delicacy: scholars seem to strongly prefer one part or the other. Jean has been called clumsy ("He is a bungler")[46] and a genius ("It is in his mastery of allegory's literary methods that he is brilliant");[47] he does not take the poetic form of allegory seriously and he uses allegory like an artist.[48]

Since, as we have noted, almost three fourths of the continuation is made up of the speeches of *auctoritas,* most attempts to evaluate Jean's use of allegory concentrate on the meaning of these speeches. Those who feel that action is the essence of allegory (Lewis, Frank) see these long speeches as digressions.[49] Others argue that it is here that Jean's brilliance manifests itself. Although there are sections of allegorical action in the second part—the battle of the pro- and contralove forces; the storming of the castle; the pilgrim's actions at the "sanctuary"— most critics see these as more contrived than the allegorical action of the first part.

The second problem is whether these personifications are speaking for the author; many scholars have made this assumption, even pulling sections out of conflicting speeches to prove "the author's point of view." Most scholars now see these speeches as part of the allegorical context, not as little lectures by Jean de Meun—language is as allegorical as action or description. The result is that more and more scholars feel that the "final meaning," if there is one, must come from the confrontation of these authorities. As Vladimir R. Rossman summed it up, "Nobody can say for sure who wins the argument, but no one can deny that both adversaries put up a good fight."[50] It is to this great debate that we now turn.

Major Personifications in the *Rose*

Reason. Lady Reason, a beautiful woman and the daughter of God, descends from her ivory tower when the Lover is in despair and tells him what a fool he is (in seventy-four lines). The Lover will not listen. She is the first personification that Jean brings back to try to set the Lover straight (this time in 4,000 lines). Again she fails. Schol-

ars divide into two camps in their explanations for this failure: some
see her as the Lover's rational will and the Lover as a sinner who will
not heed, and others argue that she is the allegorical representation of
a kind of rationality which does not know how to "reason" with a
lover.[51]

In the course of her lecture Reason covers many topics, supports her
arguments with references to the best authorities (Boethius, above all),
and illustrates them with mythological *exempla* (stories)—as do the
other voices of authority in the *Rose*. However, she discusses topics of
little interest to a man in love, such as the nonexistence of evil, and
she fails to mention the practical alternative that would make the Lover's passion acceptable to God: the sacrament of marriage. Procreation,
according to Reason, is the only acceptable goal of sexual desire; pleasure must be reduced to the unavoidable minimum. It is not surprising
that the Lover has little patience with her.

One theme recurs a number of times, becoming by force of repeti-
tion Reason's main argument against passionate love: the vagaries of
Fortune (ll. 4807ff., 5847ff., 6833ff.). Toward the end of her long
speech, Reason tries to simplify her exhortation for the poor, confused
lover—she wants just three things, that he love her, that he hate the
God of Love, and that he not value Fortune. It is the third request that
she argues for most strongly. But when she sees that she cannot win
him away from his attachment to the greatest of Fortune's gifts, love,
she offers herself as his *amie,* in a flirtatious gesture that critics have
seen as part of her feminine character (and out of character for the
personification of rationality).

Reason and the Lover disagree on many things, and the exchange
becomes lively at times, at no time more so than in their discussion of
vulgar speech (see my summary in chapter 1). When Reason tries to
raise the discussion to a higher plane by asking the Lover to look beyond the surface meaning of her words to their deeper significance (like
reading allegory—the kernel of truth beneath the shell of poetry), the
Lover replies that, frankly, he is not interested in allegorical interpretation (a remarkable statement to come from an allegorical character).
Jean has raised a number of complex issues in a few hundred lines: the
linguistic question of the relation of signifier to signified; the literary
question of allegorical language and appropriateness of characterization; the social question of class- and gender-related language differences.[52] Maureen Qulligan has called this discussion between Reason
and the Lover "the major turning point in the poem."[53] She argues that

"Jean shows that the Lover's obedience to the commandment enjoining 'clean' speech is, for allegory, a dangerous attitude, and this danger becomes the implicit subject of the rest of the poem."[54] By insisting on limiting words to their simplest, most physical meaning, the Lover destroys the possibility of moving the meaning of his experience to a more spiritual level.

This discussion of proper language (in both senses) will be one of the major items of contention in the "Querelle de la Rose" 100 years later (see chapter 4), when critics of the *Rose* will offer seven major arguments against obscene language. For, despite his obtuseness, the Lover is expressing a deep-seated human response to tabooed words, one that every society has recognized. Reason, however, sees sexuality simply as part of man's physical nature, like eating, and does not need to "gloss her words." She is unable to understand man's uneasiness, his hang-ups, about sex since the Fall. This powerlessness of Reason in the face of passion suggests a pessimistic view of human nature.

The essential questions then are: Does Reason represent Divine Sapience or is she "just" human rationality (which is inferior to faith)? Is she unquestionably right, or only partly so? The answers are vital for our understanding of the *Rose,* for if she is a rationality limited by a context with which she cannot deal, then she is simply another of the work's conflicting authorities, but if she is the correct view of the whole undertaking, as Fleming maintains, then she is not an allegorical character like the others but the voice of the author himself. Wetherbee, among others, has argued that Reason's theological limitations prevent her from understanding man's nature since the Fall.[55] And while most of the time Reason argues for the precepts of Boethian wisdom, at other times she says things that are unrighteous but reasonable, in a limited way, such as that it is better to deceive than to be deceived (ll. 4369–70; "car adés vient il mieuz, beau mestre, / decevoir que deceüz estre").

Reason's speech does not differ in form from the other characters' (even the old bawd quotes authorities, including Boethius, and offers mythological examples). Can it be argued that it differs in quality, that is, that her ideas are derived from the best and most traditional theological authorities? Is she expressing the views that Jean "must" have held, as John Fleming argues in the first chapter of *Reason and the Lover*? A number of scholars have questioned this reductive view of medieval thought (as though a learned man like Jean de Meun could only have seen things one way). We will return to this problem in chapter 5. But without getting into an analysis of the authoritativeness of Jean's sources—a complicated and lengthy undertaking—we can find evidence for the allegorical status of Reason in the structure of the *Rose* itself.

What effect does Reason's existence have on the course of the Lover's story? The answer must be none. The Lover suffers in no way because he refuses to listen to Reason; there are no consequences of this rejection indicated by the text. It could be objected that a medieval reader would of course infer the possible evil that the Lover's irrationality represented, but such a conclusion is not stated in the text. In addition, Jean himself appears to suggest that Reason does not have the final word, not only because he went on to write 15,000 post-Reason lines, but because of a remark made by the Lover after his possession of the Rose, that their seeds mixed and the Rose became larger and stretched (ll. 21689–700; the first pregnant heroine in European literature?). Thomas D. Hill has argued forcefully that this detail cannot simply be dismissed, that the fact that a child is conceived "is a significant detail which must be accounted for in any serious interpretation of the poem."[56] The Lover's foolish and sinful behavior (from Reason's point of view) results nonetheless in a great good. We must conclude, then, that Jean defines sexuality as "a profoundly paradoxical and ambivalent phenomenon."[57] Therefore, let us look at the other voices who want to have their say about it.

Nature. Mystery, goddess, philosophical concept, personification—Nature has been one of the principal intellectual challenges to which philosophers and poets have responded since the beginnings of Western thought. The complexity of this concept has led to an enormous number of definitions: Lovejoy and Boas list sixty-six meanings.[58] After Aristotle reviewed the six meanings of the term that he distinguished in his time, he proposed to define nature as "the essence of things which have in themselves, as such, a source of movement" (movement here includes growth and change).[59] Many other connotations developed in late antiquity and in the Middle Ages, especially in the twelfth century, when the Chartrian philosophers and poets placed Natura at the center of their works, in order to express their Neoplatonic views of creation. Perhaps it is in part this potential for taking on new meanings that has made the concept of Nature so appealing to poets and philosophers for so long a time.

Certain elements recur in the evolution of the term. For many thinkers, including the Greeks, Nature was the general order, the essence, of the sublunary world (time bound, deteriorating, imperfect), which they contrasted with the heavens (timeless, unchanging, perfect). Later philosophers, especially Lucretius (*De rerum natura; On the Nature of Things*), Plotinus, Chalcidius, Macrobius, and the author of the *Asclepius,* developed complex theories of nature as one of a series of intermediaries between the eternal and sublunary worlds, or between God and matter. Thus, the meanings of nature include the point of contact between the World Soul and matter, the power that brings about the creation and preservation of everything in the lower world, and, finally, the principle of order, including moral order, in this world.

In late antiquity the concept became elevated to a goddess or at least a personification (it is often difficult to determine whether an author is speaking rhetorically or theologically). Cicero describes her as endowing man with reason, Statius calls her *princeps et creatrix,* and Claudian even gives us her address (at the entrance to the cavern of *Aevum*).[60] Early Christian poets, who saw Natura as a pagan deity, insisted that the concept be limited to the creative principle that is the servant of God here below. "It is precisely this limitation and subordination of Nature," writes C. S. Lewis, "which sets her free for her triumphant poetical career. By surrendering the dull claim to be everything, she becomes somebody."[61] She becomes an important somebody in Boethius's *The Consolation of Philosophy* (see chapter 2), the work that made Nature "the most significant allegorical figure of medieval Latin and vernacular poetry."[62]

Nature, as goddess, personification, and concept, shares the functions both of Venus and of Reason—a duality that has caused difficulties.[63] As the procreative principle, Nature is often associated with Venus, who is in several works her lieutenant (in Alain de Lille's *The Plaint of Nature,* for example). This function of Nature associates her with physical desires and with feelings, thereby opposing her to Reason. Andreas Capellanus argued, in *The Art of Courtly Love,* that sins committed under the compulsion of nature could be cleansed through easy atonement (book 1, eighth dialogue). Is Nature therefore irrational (the blind procreative urge) or rational (the natural order) or both? This fundamental ambiguity underlies most of the philosophical and allegorical representations of Nature from an early period, as it underlies Jean de Meun's Nature.

She comes into the story abruptly, at line 15863, just after Venus and the God of Love swear to triumph over Chastity. At first reading, Nature's long speech, the second longest in the *Roman,* appears to be simply Jean's reworking of Alain de Lille's *The Plaint of Nature*, with little connection to the Lover's plight. But this long "confession" is neither a pedant's digression nor an example of the supposedly medieval pleasure in reworking a source, for Nature is there to answer a fundamental question: What is the place of human love in God's scheme of things? It is in order to reply to this question that Jean writes his long cosmology.

Nature's primary role is to preserve all created species from extinction by forging new individuals faster than death can grab the existing ones. Since God created the Ideas on which the species are modeled, Nature is His handmaiden, His *vicaria*. Like Alain, Jean stresses Nature's subservience to God—she can only make what is corruptible (the body), while He makes the soul. But her work is essential in God's scheme, for it continuously re-creates His original act of goodness that was the creation of the world.

All is not well in this beautiful world, however, for Nature is seen weeping over a fault that she has committed. Before we learn the nature of her "fault," we must listen to Nature's description of how every part of the universe obeys her will and God's—every part except one, man. Thus her fault is having created man. This complaint against man's unnaturalness brings Nature up against a crucial problem: Is man responsible for his waywardness? If the stars and planets affect affairs here below, and if God knows everything that is going to happen anyway, how can we hold man accountable? Nature first argues that the stars influence but do not determine man's behavior, for by use of our reason we can counteract their power. Then she reworks Boethius's discussion of free will to show how God can foresee what we will do without constraining us to do it. Divine prescience does not in any way negate man's free choice, which should be made according to reason. Thus Nature clearly aligns herself with Reason by arguing that, though we have the freedom to disobey her (which the rest of the universe does not), we should choose, reasonably, to obey her.

Nature, now our moral guide, condemns at length all the vices in which man indulges but leaves the punishment of them to God—all but one, the failure to procreate, that is, the refusal to pay one's tribute to Nature herself. Her God is here the God of the Old Testament, who orders man to be fruitful and multiply. In fact, it was to encourage men to do their duty by Nature that the sexual act was made pleasurable. Now Nature is allied with the sexual urge, with Venus (whom she calls her friend, "m'amie," l. 19313). Therefore, the function of

sexual love is to bring about the plentitude that God desires and that
was lost when Jupiter castrated Saturn (see Reason's retelling of this
myth, summarized in chapter 1).

Nature's confession raises a number of difficult questions: Is Jean
proposing a theory of "naturalism"? Does Nature go beyond Christian
orthodoxy? How does her speech prepare Genius's surprising sermon?
Why does Jean appear at times to undercut Nature's authority? Many
critics have proposed answers to the first question, without reaching
agreement (as we will see in chapter 5). Nature does base her criticism
of human vice on the Chartrian view of man as a whole being, inte-
grated into the natural as well as the spiritual world, thus implicitly
rejecting both the courtly sublimation of sexual desire and the ascetic
glorification of celibacy. But Jean's Nature goes beyond Alain de Lille's
in urging procreation as an essential part of God's plan, rather than in
simply discouraging unnatural sex. Whereas unnatural sex stood for all
the vices in the *Plaint,* procreative sex is a metaphor for all the virtues
in the *Rose.* One consequence of this broader view of sexuality is indicated by the fact that Jean's Nature does not place procreation in the
context of marriage, as Alain's Natura does.

Are Nature's views orthodox? The place of sexuality in human life
has been a difficult problem for the Catholic church, and a simple
answer to this question is not possible.[64] Briefly, sexuality was limited
to a certain context, marriage, and to a certain goal, procreation, an
acceptable one for the nonpriestly classes (though not as virtuous a goal
as continence). Jean is careful to indicate the limits in which Nature
works—she is only concerned with the natural, physical, sublunary
world and leaves all the rest to God. Thus her speech expresses a view
of sexuality that orthodox Christian theology could largely accept.

Jean also differs from Alain by greatly expanding Genius's role. Genius goes much further than Nature in urging sexual activity, for he
uses her words to build a sex-oriented view of the way to get from this
world to the next. In this way Jean again significantly changes his
"model," for Alain's Genius plays a much less important part in his
allegory, one restricted largely to carrying out Nature's instructions to
excommunicate those who sin against her.

Finally, Jean differs from Alain by appearing to undercut Nature's
authority. In the *Rose* she is much more a woman, with some of the
negative traits that medieval misogyny attributed to women, especially
talkativeness and emotionalism. Of course, it is not the author but his
character, Genius, who denounces women's failings. Nonetheless,

Nature comes through in the *Rose* with the traits that Genius claims to see in all other women. Why does Jean expand Genius's role while undercutting Nature's? Is there a connection between Genius's misogyny (women are only good for having children) and his argument that procreation is the way to Heaven? We will suggest an answer to these questions after looking at Genius's provocative sermon.

Genius. The Roman god Genius has nearly as long and as diverse a history as Nature, with whom he became associated in late antiquity. Jane Chance Nitzsche summarizes the "bewilderingly diverse array" of Genius's forms and associations in *The Genius Figure in Antiquity and the Middle Ages.*[65] Originally a spirit of begetting, specifically the reproductive power of the *paterfamilias,* Genius later came to be seen as the tutelary god of every man, his *animus* or life force, which he was encouraged to indulge with wine and food, especially on his birthday (the origin of our birthday parties). Genius also came to stand for human nature and its potential, for man's rational soul, or his good and evil impulses. Finally, various *genii* were associated with the World Soul, with stars and planets (and therefore with Fortune), and with demons.

It is perhaps relevant to Jean de Meun's conception of his character Genius that from the earliest period Genius was associated solely with male procreation (Nitzsche argues that a woman's personal god was Juno). From the god of the male head of household, Genius became the god of any man, married or unmarried. Moving from a man's loins to his head, the individual man's genius came to represent his rational soul, then his unique qualities, given to him at birth by his stars. Finally, there developed the modern concept of great mental capacity or inventive ability, especially great and original creative talent. This evolution shows a clear pattern of intellectualization that moves from virility to higher and higher mental gifts, as if sexuality and intellectual ability were ultimately linked.

Jean's Genius is both a god of generation and, like Alain de Lille's Genius, Nature's priest and therefore presumably a moral guide. These two functions are linked from his first appearance (ll. 16242–54), in which Genius is celebrating mass in his chapel, a mass that consists of "reciting" the individual forms based on the models that Nature has given him. And as both her priest and the "god and master of the sexual organs" (ll. 16256), he is instructed to excommunicate, before the hosts of the God of Love, all those who sin against Nature's law.

Genius's relation to Venus and her son is more ambiguous. What does it mean that the God of Love dresses him in bishop's robe and insignia after Genius has taken off the habit of Nature's priest? Or that Venus, laughing gaily, hands Genius a burning taper that "n'estoit pas de cire vierge" (l. 19460; was not of virgin wax)? Is the God of Love making use of the procreative urge for his own purposes, or does Genius know that even courtly love can serve his procreative ends? Who is using whom? In any case, at this point, love, courtly or lustful, is clearly allied with procreation.

The sermon that Genius pronounces falls into two parts, each based roughly on the two parts of Nature's instructions to him: excommunicate those who do not serve her, promise full pardon to those who repent of their sins against her. Genius takes each part a step further: he urges unrestrained procreation, thereby making a relative good (reproduction of the species) into the ultimate value, and he promises Heaven itself to those who follow him. Thus we are told that there is no higher value than procreation and that there is no higher reward than the one that awaits good procreators.

Genius addresses briefly the question of chastity, a virtue that church doctrine placed above procreation (ll. 19569–98). Why, he asked, if chastity is the surer road to Heaven, and if God loves us all equally, does He not instruct us all to remain chaste? Although Genius sidesteps an answer ("Go ask a theologian," he says), his rhetorical questions and his concern that generation would cease suggest that he rejects continence. He even goes so far as to call for the castration of all those who do not use their "tools," although later he condemns castration as a sin against the individual, masculinity (it makes men like women, who are ready to do any devilry), and Nature.

The value of continence was a question that much concerned Christian thinkers at the time Jean de Meun was writing the *Rose*. St. Thomas, for example, takes up the problem both in his *Contra Gentiles* and the *Summa theologiae*.[66] In 1277 a series of propositions was condemned by the bishop of Paris, several of which questioned the virtue of continence or even claimed that it was a hindrance to virtue. These propositions were generally attributed to a group of young scholars today called heterodox Aristotelians, for their radical acceptance of Aristotelian and Averroïst ideas. Some scholars believe that Jean was sympathetic to these views, or even a fervent adherent.[67] This would mean, however, that Jean, who is conservative up to Genius's speech (in his support of the university authorities through the character of False Seeming, for example), becomes a radical in sexual doctrine. It will be clear from the following discussion that this contradiction does not exist. But Genius is certainly referring to the debate on celibacy, and although he does not pronounce directly on the question, he indirectly discredits chastity by extolling procreation. "Arez, por Dieu, baron, arez, et voz lignages reparez" (ll. 19671–72; Plow, for God's sake, barons, plow, and repair your lignage).

To encourage his listeners in their efforts to serve Nature, Genius describes, in twice as many words as the first part of the sermon, the wondrous Heaven that awaits those who follow him, which he calls the "parc du champ joli" (l. 19905; the Park of the lovely field, or, as critics often refer to it, of the Good Shepherd). To this apotheosis of the medieval literary garden, in which little lambs frolic among ever-blooming flowers, Genius adds many Christian symbols representing the unity of the Trinity, the Crucifixion, and Christ's tender concern for his "sheep." Finally, he contrasts this garden, point for point, to that of the God of Love, to show the barons how greatly this one is to be desired.

Thus the two parts of Genius's sermon represent the two functions that he fulfills in medieval allegorical works, god of generation, and tutelary spirit or moral guide. Jean has his Genius play the two roles consecutively, rather than simultaneously, as Alain de Lille's Genius does, and this split has also divided critical thinking on the meaning of Genius's sermon. No interpretation has yet been proposed that unifies these two disparate messages, the naturalistic exhortation to procreation and the pious description of the Park of the Good Shepherd. Critics who see Genius (and often Jean de Meun, too) as sympathetic to a kind of pagan naturalism emphasize the first part of the sermon while avoiding consideration of the religious vision. This naturalism is then judged as either admirable or evil.[68] Others, wanting to see Genius as a moral guide, minimize the sexual message in various ways, such as by setting up an analogy between human and divine love, but this interpretation does not explain the incongruity of a learned medieval writer using, not human love, but the procreative act as a metaphor for God's grace.[69]

These paradoxical parts of the sermon come together if we see Genius as the satiric portrait of a popular preacher, of whom there were many in the thirteenth century. The tone of the sermon is one of persuasion, not of dispassionate exposition. For example, when Genius has finished his comparison of the two gardens, he calls on the barons to choose between them: "Pour Dieu, seigneur, donc que vos samble / du

parc et du jardin ansamble?" (ll. 20567–68; In God's name, my lords,
how does it seem to you, comparing the park and the garden?) This
wonderful Park is used to win over his listeners, not simply so that
they will follow his teaching but so they will also spread the "good
word." For just before Genius describes his Heaven, he asks his audience to go out and preach for him (ll. 19896–905): My lady Nature
needs preachers; if you preach for her, you will go to Heaven. Thus
Genius's rhetoric is skillfully designed to attain a proselytizing goal.

The satire grows out of the way Genius will use any demogogic
method in his power to accomplish his ends. Like a street vendor he
exclaims on the wonderful worth of his "product," in a hyperbolic bit
of self-praise: "Ma parole est mout vertueuse, / ele est .c. tanz plus
precieuse / que safir, rubiz ne balai" (ll. 19893–95; My word is very
powerful, it is a hundred times more precious than saphire, ruby, precious stone). But he also uses more subtle means to win assent. We
have already described how he manipulates the audience's attitude toward chastity. His references to the Christian virtues and vices illustrate the same desire to manipulate. When first discussing the vices
they should rid themselves of, Genius sends his listeners to read about
them in the *Roman de la rose*! And when he exhorts them to lead a good
life, he quickly defines that life as embracing one's lover.

Genius finally gets around to naming some of the virtues necessary
for entering Heaven, tossing off a short, eclectic list that includes pay-
ing one's debts (if one has the cash), avoiding murder, and keeping
one's hands and mouth clean (no mention of loving God, however) (ll.
19835–866, 20597–629). Clearly Genius demands little from his followers, except that they be "es euvres naturex / plus vistes que nus
escurex" (ll. 19659–60; quicker than squirrels to do the work of
nature).

Jean has created the satiric portrait of a demagogic preacher who has
taken an idea (procreation has a function in the natural order) to an
extreme (procreation is the only good), a monomaniac who has some
familiarity with current theological disputes and much skill in rhetorical manipulation. Only Alan Gunn has recognized the specific satiric
nature of this character, but he does not consider the consequences of
this interpretation for our understanding of Genius's message.[70] Scholars, including Gunn, have focused on one or another aspect of Genius's
message or on its literary or cultural context; they have not looked at
the way this message is realized in this particular character. It is nec-

essary to understand what Jean is doing with the character in order to judge Genius's credibility as an authority on love.

Jean is not advocating naturalism, nor is Genius simply an allegorical manifestation of concupiscence. He is a skillful example of how ideas can be manipulated in the service of a cause. Rather than supporting the ideas of the heterodox Aristotelians, Jean is ridiculing these new ideas based on reason alone. Thus, this interpretation of Genius is further support for the critical view that Jean's characters are not speaking for him, that his view of allegory is profoundly satiric, and that the message cannot be separated from its source. Many of Genius's ideas could be valid in other contexts, but we must look at the use he puts them to. Scholars have not yet dealt with this question of the relation of the medium to the message: if Genius's sermon is demogogery, can we accept anything he says as expressing the author's views? If Jean's work is a mirror, as he claims, the images it reflects are distorted, inverted for ironic purposes, like those reflections that Nature discusses in what has been considered a digression, but that can now be seen to be a key to Jean's artistic method (see ll. 18004–30).

This approach to Genius suggests a new interpretation of two problematic passages of the last part of the *Rose*, Genius's misogynistic outburst to Nature and the Lover's rape of the sanctuary while disguised as a pilgrim. Genius interjects a passage of violent attack on woman, the "venimeuse beste" (l. 16577; venomous beast), before he hears Nature's confession. After hundreds of lines of invective, he adds, almost as an afterthought, that all this should not stop a man from lying with women in order to continue his species. How galling to Genius to realize that the ultimate good, procreation, is not really in the control of men at all, that man, whom he believes to be the active force in generation (women wait passively for the stylus, hammer, or ploughshare) must depend on another human being, one who too often appears to have a mind of her own. His misogynistic view of women is therefore a result of his reducing them to their procreative function.

Finally, we come to a passage that readers have found to be disturbing, the Lover's forceful penetration of the "sanctuary" with his staff. It has been suggested that Jean is wittily turning courtly euphemism against its supporters (the Lover, who objected to the use of obscene words, carries out an obscene act in the guise of polite metaphor). While this may be part of what Jean is suggesting, the fact that this passage comes soon after Genius's sermon, in which unbridled sexuality is disguised as pious behavior, gives the Lover's deed new meaning. The pilgrim-lover's actions at the sanctuary are a metaphor for what the demogogue Genius has done to ideas; he has covered them with religious trappings in order to distort, to violate, them.

Chapter Four
The Influence of
the *Roman de la rose*

Because of its popularity the *Roman de la rose* exerted an enormous influence on European literature: more than any other medieval work it changed the way writers thought about certain subjects, such as love, nature, and the potential of verse narrative. The *Rose*'s influence was greatest in France and England, where poets like Machaut, Villon, Chaucer, and Spenser knew the work so well that it became part of their poetic vocabulary. In this chapter I will outline the influence of the *Rose* in France, England, and Italy. I will also discuss the literary debate it provoked at the end of the fourteenth century.

The Seeds of the *Rose*

The presence of the *Rose* is visible in a gamut of literary works in passages that range from translations to vague echoes. Between these extremes we find many works of prosification, "moralization," and other forms of commentary, excerpts of a few lines or of whole passages, references brief or extended to one or both parts of the *Rose,* imitations of form or subject matter, adaptations (including one sonnet cycle), and paraphrases of major ideas. Furthermore, the influence of the work extended beyond France through translations into English, Flemish, German, and Italian. To repeat C. S. Lewis's remark, "The poems that derive from it constitute the most important literary phenomenon of the later Middle Ages. As a germinal book during these centuries it ranks second to none except the Bible and the *Consolation of Philosophy*."[1] Thirty years later John V. Fleming reaffirmed that the *Roman* "is the most important (in the sense of being the most widely-read and most influential) vernacular poem of the Middle Ages."[2]

Thus, because of the time period, the geographical area, and the number of works involved, the subject of the influence of the *Rose* is an enormous one. It is also a subject made more difficult by the problem of determining kinds of influence in late medieval literature, where no work stands alone. I discussed in chapter 2 how medieval authors saw their works as responses to earlier works and how they adapted those works to their own purposes. The same problems of determining the relation of the *Rose* to its sources arise when we study the works that the *Rose* supposedly influenced. The presence of similar verses in the *Rose* and later works does not necessarily indicate a direct influence—we need to look for exact phrases (that could not be the result of chance) or larger narrative elements and ideas. Our findings will remain largely tentative, however, for the influence of the *Rose* may in many cases have been an indirect one.

There are few close imitations of the *Rose* in the centuries following it, that is, few extended allegories that suggest the long, subtle unfolding of a love story. Poets do, however, incorporate many of its elements, such as the allegorical personifications, the setting, or the questions about the nature of love. They break up the complex equilibrium of the *Rose* and recompose some of its components into new combinations. C. S. Lewis describes the *Rose* as a parent who begets offspring "at once like and unlike itself."[3] This potential for suggesting new answers to the same literary questions may be one of the principal reasons for the enormous popularity of the *Rose*.

France

For two and half centuries most love poems written in France were influenced to some degree by the *Roman de la rose*.[4] In order to see how poets responded to the allegory of love in Guillaume de Lorris's *Rose*, we will look at a number of poems that incorporate the elements of the autobiographical dream in order to re-create the allegorical story of a young man in love.

The dream poem was one of the most popular types of late medieval narratives (Chaucer, Langland, Lydgate, and many others wrote dream poems), in part perhaps because of the example of the *Rose*. Although the dream poem was used in the early Middle Ages to express religious experiences, the *Rose* caused the dream setting to be associated mainly with an allegorical love adventure. (See chapter 2, above, for a discussion of the dream poem before the *Rose*.) According to Badel, it was thanks to the *Rose* that "le songe allégorique devenait pour plus de deux siècles le cadre poétique préféré des créateurs" (the allegorical dream became for more than two centuries the frame preferred by creators).[5]

A. C. Spearing has made some perceptive suggestions to account for this popularity. One of the most important is that the dream framework allows the poet to express his consciousness of himself as a poet and to make his work reflexive.[6] The dream framework was a door to allegory, to the garden of love—to a mysterious Other World.[7]

One of the first examples of the love poem set as a dream is *Li Fablel dou Dieu d'Amors* (The fable of the God of Love), an anonymous work from the second half of the thirteenth century. Scholars originally thought that it was a major source of the *Rose* (see chapter 2, n. 17), but it is now believed to have been written after the first part of the *Rose*. It is a good example of how later poems adapted elements from the *Rose*.

In a short prologue to the *Fablel* the poet calls on his audience of "franch chevalier, baron, dames, puceles" to listen to his "avision". One morning in May he was lying awake in his bed, thinking of love, when he had the following dream, which made him very happy. In the dream it is also a May morn, and the birds are singing. The dreamer-narrator strolls through a meadow full of flowers, through which flows a stream whose waters keep one forever young and also restore a maiden's virginity. He comes to an orchard, the door of which is always closed "vilains" (commoners) but open to "cortois" (nobles)—the poet points out that *he* has no difficulty entering. There he finds 100,000 birds, each singing of love as it understands it. His heart is so filled with joy that he believes himself to be in paradise. He listens to the birds discuss the nature of love, and when they go home to their nests, this first dream ends. But the poet promises to tell also the dream that followed if someone will give him a drink.

In the second dream, the dreamer, still in the meadow, sees his beloved arrive. They embrace and affirm their love for each other. Suddenly, a great winged serpent swoops down and makes off with the damsel. The lover is about to kill himself when up rides the God of Love on a horse covered with flowers; he is wearing a robe made of springtime, bird calls, kisses, and hugs. Love, promising to help him, takes him to his castle, then rides off in pursuit of the lady. The castle is described in detailed allegorical terms: it is made of sighs and tears, sweet loving and service, all held together by Breton lais and songs, and a phoenix guards the door. After answering the phoenix's riddle ("What was born without a mother?"), the lover is warmly received by the God's followers. Despite his distraught frame of mind, he sings them a song. A damsel tells him the sad story of how she lost her lover, who is buried in a nearby field (the story of how he was killed by an arrogant knight is like a scene from a Breton romance). The God of Love returns with the maiden, an event that fills the lover with great joy—unlike what he feels in "real life" (where evidently his beloved is much less friendly). This great joy awakens him, and he realizes sadly that the whole dream was a lie.

A number of elements of the *Fablel* probably derive from the *Rose*, including the dream framework; the season and the setting, with its orchard, flowers, and birds; and the character of the God of Love. The two poems also have similar conceptions of the roles of the God of Love and the lover. The God of Love plays an active part in the *Fablel* as he does in the *Rose*, while the lover is for the most part passive. In fact, lovers become more and more passive in late medieval poems. In the *Oit de la Panthère d'amors* (The Panther of Love), for example, the lover does little except lie abed and complain about how passive he is. In the *Roman de la poire* (The romance of the pear) the lover refuses to speak to his lady even after the urging of Pitié and four other messengers from the God of Love.[8] Despite these borrowings, there are significant differences between the two poems.

Like the *Fablel,* many French poems of the late Middle Ages pick up certain elements from the *Rose* and adapt them to a new love story. The dream framework, for example, provided poets with the chance to introduce variations on the basic pattern. Among the variables found in dream poems are the truth or falsehood of the dream, and the ways in which the dreamer falls asleep or awakes.[9] In the *Rose* the lover simply tells us that he had a dream, but later writers talk about thinking of their beloved before falling asleep, thereby relating their waking thoughts to the dream content (as Chaucer does in *The Parlement of Fowls*).

One of the most original variations in the awakening is found in Guillaume de Machaut's *Dit dou vergier* (orchard or garden): the God of Love accidentally showers dew down on the dreamer, thereby waking him in a way that interlocks dream and reality, for the imaginary dew falls on the dreamer from the real tree under which he is dreaming.[10] Machaut, the most skillful lyric poet in French before Villon, wrote a number of long love poems, the most important of which are the *Dit dou vergier,* the *Jugement dou roy de Behaingne* (The King of Bohemia's verdict), and the *Voir dit* (The true story). His poems show a subtle reworking of the conception of love found in the *Rose*.[11]

Birds are another common element of love poems after the *Rose*, and one that shows much variation. In the *Messe des oiseaux,* for example, the dreamer listens to the birds discuss the nature of love, then sing a Mass. But the poet of the *Echecs d'amour* (Love's chess game) complains that the reason his poem is not a dream is that the loud singing of the birds kept him awake![12]

Thus the *Fablel,* one of the earliest works to show the influence of Guillaume de Lorris's *Rose,* has picked up many of the elements of setting and character that later works will also incorporate. But the differences between the *Fablel* and the *Rose* are significant also. In the *Fablel* there is no sustained allegory, no allegorical characters other than the God of Love. Furthermore, there are no philosophical discussions, no instruction in the art of love, no allegorical enemies to come between the lovers. Finally, a significant divergence is indicated by the presence of a beloved of flesh and blood in the *Fablel,* not a symbolic one.

Late medieval love poems as a whole, while incorporating many elements found in the *Rose,* often do not follow the earlier work in its portrayal of female characters. The beloved and Venus in particular differ from their ancestors in the *Rose.* The beloved is rarely allegorized (the Lady in the *Roman de la poire,* despite the title, is not a pear). The only major work from this period to present an allegorical object of love is the *Panthère d'amors,* in which the beloved is a panther, with the symbolic qualities attributed to it in the bestiaries (its breath, for example, cures all ills). Thus the lovers' ladies in late allegorical poems become more realistic and usually more accepting of the lover than was Guillaume de Lorris's Rose.

Venus also becomes less allegorical, more realistic—she is no longer the powerful, flame-throwing goddess of the *Rose,* but a wise and kind courtly lady. In the *Panthère d'amors,* she sits by the suffering lover's bed and gently encourages him to speak to his beloved. When she appears at all in the later works, she has been demoted from the God of Love's superior to his wife. Finally, Nature and Reason do not appear in the allegorical love poems (except for the *Echecs d'amour*), but they are taken up by the philosophical or satiric poems influenced by the second part of the *Rose.*

Thus the *Fablel,* the *Panthère d'amors,* and other works of this period show us a narrative approach that appears to have been common practice in the late Middle Ages, that is, to pull out from the *Rose* only those elements that interested the author—and since there was so much from which to choose, the works influenced by the *Rose* are very variable. Muscatine has observed that Guillaume's imitators take variously "the erotic content, the setting, the actors, the superficial prettiness, but not the basic structure."[13] Wimsatt, on the other hand, categorizes love poems after Guillaume according to their relation to the three major sections of the first part of the *Rose,* first the Maytime walk to and through the Garden of Deduit, then a series of love experiences, finally a full-blown psychological allegory.[14] Poets after Guillaume found innumerable variations of these basic motifs.

Despite these poetic traditions, however, later poems do not borrow the *Rose's* pessimistic view of love's chances. The agonistic element is almost eliminated, and the lover often achieves fairly quickly what he desires. In Machaut's *Dit dou vergier,* for instance, the lover's supporters, who include Grace, Pitié, Esperance, and Souvenir, simply persuade Dangiers to allow the lover "La joie qui est nompareille" (the joy that is without equal). By following the changes that later poets make in what they borrow from the *Rose,* we can see how French love poetry was evolving in the fourteenth and fifteenth centuries away from Guillaume de Lorris's view of love as an awesome or profound experience.

Jean de Meun's influence is seen not in the development of allegories of love but in the many philosophical, moral, and satiric works of the fourteenth and fifteenth centuries, including even animal fables such as *Renard le Contrefait.*[15] The *Rose* was the first text in French to serve widely as a literary model for narrative technique, style, and theme.

The vogue in allegorical and didactic literature of this period for writing "par personnages" is largely a result of Jean's successful creation, or re-creation, of types like False Seeming, the Jealous Husband, and the Old Woman. Three of the four earliest mentions of the *Rose* are references to a particular character.[16] Writers after the *Rose* tended to adopt its satiric characters whose importance is suggested by the fact that medieval writers often referred to the characters in the *Rose* as "chapters": "le chapitre de Faux Semblant," for example. They saw the *Rose* as structured by these characters whom Jean de Meun, if he did not create them all, nonetheless cast in their definitive form.

Traditional themes, myths, and images were also given a new popularity by the second part of the *Rose.* The fourteenth century knew many fables and ancient stories in the form that Jean de Meun gave them. His version of the story of Lucretia, for example (ll. 8578–8621), became the accepted version for many writers. The use of pagan myths and stories becomes widespread in vernacular literature after Jean de Meun. But the *Rose* was also seen as a reservoir of ideas and metaphors (the fecundity of nature, the value of "sufficiency," the nobility of the heart, woman as serpent). In addition, the *Rose* gave writers ways of expressing some of the most popular subjects of satire, that of estates and conditions. In other words, the *Rose* became "an authority" like the works of the classical writers on which it drew. Writers drew from the *Rose* as Jean de Meun had drawn from earlier writers like Cicero and Boethius. And the fourteenth century saw the same kind of studies of Jean's sources as were done for classical writers.[17]

But these images, stories, characters, and other materials taken from the *Rose* were rarely used to express the same ideas as they had for Jean de Meun. Thus they appear to us out of context (just as Jean himself had incorporated materials out of context; see Thomas D. Hill's discussion of the Old Woman's "digression on free love").[18] In general, Jean's successors, who were much more conservative than he, evidently saw no difficulty in using his words to express very different views— the fourteenth-century abbot, Gilles le Muisis, for example, celebrates chastity but admires the *Roman de la rose* nonetheless: "J'ay pau trouvet plus bielle chose / Que c'est dou *Romanc de le Rose*" (I have rarely found a more beautiful thing than the *Romance of the rose*).[19] This fragmented use of parts of the *Rose* suggests, not that medieval readers had a coherent, unified view of the author's "message," but that they selected from the romance phrases, themes, images that supported their own ideas.

The profoundest influence that Jean de Meun exercised on subsequent French literature, and European literature generally, was to offer a new understanding of the potential of vernacular literature to treat a wide range of topics. Poets became more ambitious in the treatment of philosophical and moral subjects in the context of works on love— love was seen as a path to wisdom. Jean de Meun's erudition showed later writers that works in the popular languages could reach the same learned level as those in Latin, that their style could show the same rhetorical and poetic beauty. It is in this new view of literature, rather than in the borrowing of specific elements, that Jean's work permanently changed European literature. (See the discussion of Dante below.)

The *Rose* also influenced the early development of literary criticism through a debate on its merits, now called the "Querelle (quarrel) de la Rose," which developed at the beginning of the fifteenth century and which consisted of an exchange of letters, sermons, and an allegorical treatise.[20] Three men argued in support of the *Rose*: Jean de

Montreuil, provost of Lille and secretary to dukes and kings; Gontier Col, first secretary and notary to King Charles VI of France; and his brother, Pierre, canon of Paris and Tournay. They were answered by two people: one of the most notable clerics of the period, Jean Gerson, chancellor of the University of Paris, and a woman, Christine de Pizan, the author of a large number of poetic works, allegories, and treatises. Christine de Pizan was in fact the most energetic of the participants, for she wrote more than all the others combined, and she made the debate public by sending copies of some of the letters to the queen.[21] There are indications that the debate was of interest to a broad public of nobility and bourgeoisie.[22]

The fundamental question raised by Gerson and de Pizan was nothing less than the moral responsibility of writers. They pointed to the use of obscene language and the exhortations to fornication (whose other side was the condemnation of chastity) as reprehensible even in a work of fiction. In addition, Christine rejected the misogynistic views expressed in the work. Although they agreed with Pierre Col that characters must speak in an appropriate manner (the ancient principle of "decorum"), they refused to allow this principle to excuse immoral or blasphemous writing.[23]

The defenders of the *Rose* offered arguments that, while carrying some weight in themselves, tended to contradict each other: they argued, for example, that we must look beyond the author's words to his intentions but that we must stick to the text when judging his words. Pierre Col's letter to Christine, for example (no. 13, *Querelle*), argues for interpreting Jean's words: "One must not take words literally in this way, but rather according to what was previously said and the intention of the author," but two pages later he asserts that in the speech of the Jealous Husband Jean was simply showing what a jealous husband is like. In any case, the *Rose*'s defenders argued, Jean's views were completely moral; where he appears to be urging immoral principles, he is simply telling us what not to do.

Though no agreement was reached (Pierre Col stopped replying after he realized the seriousness of Gerson's condemnation of his views), this long literary debate changed the way people read the *Rose*; it could no longer be accepted as a unified, consistently orthodox text. Nonetheless, it continued to be read, sympathetically for the most part, for a century and a half, both by educated people generally and by poets such as François Villon and Clément Marot.

It is a truism of French literary history that François Villon was the first "modern" French poet because he brings a more personal vision to the traditional themes of medieval poetry. Many of these themes are central to the *Rose,* also, but scholars have not found agreement on the question of Villon's debt to the *Rose* (as they have not for Chaucer or Dante either): Louis Thuasne has argued most strongly for Villon's links with Jean de Meun; Italo Siciliano limits this influence to the two "Belle Heaumière" poems (see below); André Lanly takes the most balanced view but maintains nonetheless "que Villon connaissait bien certaines oeuvres de Jean de Meun et qu'il en a subi l'influence" (that Villon knew well certain works of Jean de Meun and that he was influenced by them).[24] The problem again results from the fact that medieval writers, even those separated by centuries, shared a common literary and philosophical culture. Although it is not possible to establish precisely how Villon was affected by the *Rose,* it is clear that he was familiar with it and that many of the themes that were of concern to Jean de Meun concerned him also.

Villon suggests this familiarity directly by the reference to Jean de Meun as a satirist of the Mendicant Orders: "Maistre Jehan de Meun s'en mocqua / De leur façon" (Master Jean de Meun mocked their behavior).[25] He mentions the "noble Romant de la Rose,"[26] although here Villon appears to be referring to the opening of a work usually attributed to Jean de Meun, also called the *Testament* (see chapter 1). This supposed last will and testament of Jean de Meun, as well as the will that the Lover makes at the end of the first part, may very well have shaped Villon's decision to write in the genre of the literary will. It appears, though, that Villon's knowledge of the *Rose* was superficial. He had inherited the courtly vocabulary and images of Guillaume de Lorris (but probably mainly through his successors) as well as certain themes, such as that of Fortune, and the satiric references to the Mendicant Orders, but these were all part of a common poetic culture in the late Middle Ages to which Villon gives a more fearful, obsessional tone.

Where Villon does show that he thought about a character in the *Rose* in an original manner is in his inspired portrait of an Old Woman. Placed among the ballads in which Villon laments the degradation that time causes are two poems spoken by his most memorable creation, the once-desirable woman called "la belle Heaumière" (helmet-maker). Both her lament, "Les regrets de la belle Heaumière," and the following ballad in which she gives advice to young "filles de joie" (prostitutes), show her to be a descendant of Jean de Meun's Old Woman.

All of the major themes woven into the Old Woman's speech to
Warm Welcome are picked up by Villon and reworked in a way that
expresses the cultural changes that have occurred in the 150 years since
the death of Jean de Meun. These themes include the need to enjoy
pleasure while youth and beauty last, the ugly changes in the female
body that time brings, a woman's lustfulness and her irrational attachment to a man who mistreats her, the natural freedom of a woman to
love whomever she chooses, her need to instruct younger women, and
finally her desire to use sexual favors for gain, both to insure a com-
fortable old age and to avenge herself on the men who use her for
pleasure when she was young but who discarded her now she is old.
Jean de Meun links, in his Old Woman's speech, the two themes of
bitter regret for the way men have treated her and instruction in venality by having the first motivate the second.

The inspiration for this character is usually given as Ovid's Dipsas,
a *lena* (procuress) who is the subject of elegy 8 of the *Amores*. But
neither Jean de Meun's nor Villon's old woman is a go-between (a common character in drama and narrative since the Greeks; see, for example, the old procuress called "Buen Amor" in Juan Ruiz's *Libro de Buen
Amor* and the old woman in the Latin work *Pamphilus*). The old women
in the *Rose* and the *Testament* do not help men seduce women for pay,
as the procuress does; they even appear to be harming the seducer's
interests by urging women to make him pay. The refrain of Villon's
"Ballade aux Filles de Joie" is that since an old woman is worth no
more than devalued money, she should sell her goods while they have
value. But the old woman's regret that she did not profit from men's
attentions when she had the "commodity" to sell is simply another way
for a poet to accuse women of wanting to make money from sex—the
old procuress sells young women, while young women sell themselves.
(The connection between the two ideas is also suggested by the fact
that Ovid's procuress teaches the young woman how to "pluck" the
lover.) Both variants of this character appear to fascinate writers, while
also disgusting them, for they have returned to the Old Woman again
and again.

Jean's Old Woman also suggests the theme of "carpe diem" through
her laments on her lost beauty. She describes the great power that
beauty gave her over men, but she suggests only briefly the sad state
in which old age has placed her. One of the principle developments
that Villon brought to this character was the long, detailed description
of her physical deterioration: "What has become of that smooth fore-

head and blond hair, that beautiful straight nose, red lips, small breasts, little sex in its little garden?" and so on for five stanzas. Villon follows the conventional order of the description of feminine beauty in medieval literature (from head to foot) but turns over the beautiful image to show the rot underneath: "C'est d'humaine beauté l'issue!" (This is the outcome of human beauty!). He thus elaborates, in a moving way, a theme of late medieval and Renaissance literature, the transience of human life, epitomized by the rapid fading of a woman's beauty. After her beauty is gone, she in effect no longer exists. While Jean only touches on the theme: "quant vostre rose iert flestrie" (l. 14514; when your rose will have wilted), Villon stresses the process of physical deterioration that so obsessed the late Middle Ages.[27]

But at least, exclaims the Old Woman, "ai je ma joie eüe" (l. 12913; I have had my joy). From the lover's point of view, perhaps, he feels less like a fool if, for paid pleasures, he has given pleasure in return. Thus the two themes of women's avariciousness and lust are always intertwined. In order to see her as more human, perhaps, scholars have unfortunately stressed the lustfullness of Jean's Old Woman and ignored her venality, a sin condemned in the strongest terms by Guillaume's God of Love (ll. 10735–96).[28] Does her lustful nature make her more likeable? Isn't lust the least serious of the sins in Dante's *Purgatorio?* Lust is, after all, an excess of love, of a kind, for another human being. But it is necessary to recognize the old woman's venality, which is the object of both stern moral condemnation and a movement of sympathy for the social vulnerability of the woman who grows old outside marriage. Jean de Meun and Villon appear to have perceived, if unconsciously, the evil that men do to women whom they seduce and abandon and women's need to protect themselves.

The fascination of this character for medieval writers did not die with Villon. Chaucer, for example, created a cousin of these old women in the Wife of Bath. A cousin, not a sister, for there are important differences between her and her ancestors. Chaucer has made his character more middle class, more respectable, by marrying her to middle-class husbands. She is just as avaricious, however, just as duplicious, as her unmarried and therefore more vulnerable sisters. Chaucer uses the Wife of Bath very cleverly to repeat the traditional misogynistic charges by having her tell us what she said to her husbands when they accused her of all those terrible things (accusations that echo those of Jean de Meun's Jealous Husband). But she offers much more than another satire of women, for the satiric character reacts very humanly to her own portrait and destroys it by throwing into the fire her husband's book of writings against women (causing readers who are both women and scholars to cheer and weep at the same time).

Chaucer has made a second significant change in the Wife by having her accept her "old age" with good-natured optimism. She does not even see it as a handicap, for she hopes soon to have yet another husband. But like her ancestors she sees femininity as a commodity that, if used astutely, will get her what she wants. And she understands better than they what they really want—power over men.

Thus all three of these old women are like lightning rods that draw to themselves some of men's deepest fears about life and death. Perhaps this is why the Old Woman as a literary character has fascinated writers for so long.

A century after Villon the influence of the *Rose* on French writers had nearly disappeared (see the discussion in chapter 5 of criticism in the sixteenth and seventeenth centuries). Eighteenth-century writers, on the contrary, began reading the *Rose* and responding to some of the major themes of the second part, according to recent research by French scholars, notably Jean-Charles Payen.[29] New editions of the *Rose* brought it to the attention of the *philosophes,* who found in it many of the same preoccupations that concerned their age: the question of the institution of property, of the "noble savage," of the human potential for good or evil. Jean-Jacques Rousseau, who quotes two lines from the *Rose* in *La nouvelle Heloïse,* was concerned throughout his life with these social questions. But a direct influence of the *Rose* on Rousseau's political thought is still hypothetical, for there is no strong textual evidence that Rousseau was thinking of the *Rose* when he wrote the *Discours* or the *Contrat social.* The themes that his works share with the *Rose* were found in other works, such as those of Montaigne, with whom Rousseau was familiar. It is unlikely that Rousseau or Diderot were led to their philosophical views by Jean de Meun, but it is certainly possible that they had read the *Rose* and found in it support for their own thinking on certain questions.

England

The influence of the *Rose* on English literature is nearly as great as its influence on French literature. Most works on love, allegorical or not, from Gower to Milton, pick up and modify the traditions expressed in the *Rose.* The character Genius, for example, reappears in

Gower's *Confessio Amantis* (The lover's confession), in which a lover whom Guillaume de Lorris would have admired confesses his sins, amorous and other, to a new version of Jean's Genius. The structure of the *Confessio Amantis* could also have been influenced by Jean's *Rose,* for it incorporates scientific lectures, moral discussions, and illustrative stories.

Jean de Meun's great character Genius becomes, in Gower's work, Venus's priest rather than Nature's, and this change has challenged scholars to understand and explain it. While it is true that Jean's Genius is in effect one of Venus's allies (she laughingly hands him her candle in a gesture that seems to make him her priest), nonetheless Gower's Genius is a moral philosopher very different from Jean's. The Venus he serves, consequently, is probably the "good" Venus of which Natura speaks in Alain de Lille's *The Plaint of Nature,* Venus before her revolt against Nature's rule. Thus the major characters in the *Rose* continued to inspire poets to rethink them at least until the Renaissance.[30]

One of the greatest medieval writers inspired by the *Rose* was Geoffrey Chaucer. For a hundred years scholars have been trying to evaluate Chaucer's "lifelong use" of the *Rose* (to quote Charles Muscatine), from the earliest works, such as the "complaints," to the *Canterbury Tales.* But Chaucer's works echo the *Rose* so subtly, at times so elusively, that no definitive study of the relationship has been yet achieved.[31] Agreement has been reached, however, on certain general areas of influence, which I will summarize in this section.

Chaucer himself gives us direct evidence that he has "absorbed the *Roman* into his very bones"[32] through three explicit references to it and his mention of his own translation. In the *Book of the Duchess,* the poet dreams that he awakens in a marvelous chamber, on the walls of which are painted in fine colors not only the *Roman de la rose* but its gloss (is Chaucer thus glossing the dream he is about to recount?). Many details of the dream—the May morning, the singing of the birds, the wonderful forest where the narrator finds the Black Knight—echo Guillaume de Lorris's dream.[33] Furthermore, Chaucer treats the *Rose* as if it were the epitome of literary genius, for in "The Merchant's Tale" he claims that even the author (*sic*) of the *Romance of the rose* would not be able to well describe the beauty of January's garden; thus does Chaucer excuse himself for not even trying.

It is in the prologue to the *Legend of Good Women* that Chaucer makes his most extended reference to the *Rose.* In the dream that frames this poem, the God of Love appears—on a May morning, in a beautiful meadow, accompanied by the singing of many birds—but when he learns to whom he is speaking, his mood grows wintry. The dreamer is angrily accused of having translated a work that is heresy to Love's religion—none other than the *Romance of the rose.*

In fact, we possess three fragments of a Middle English translation of the *Rose* (equaling about one third of the original), which was at first believed entirely by Chaucer (following Thynne, the editor of the 1532 edition), then that none of it was his work, now that the first fragment was probably his.[34] This fragment stops at line 1705, when the God of Love is shooting the Lover with his arrows, but the God in the prologue to the *Legend of Good Women* is certainly referring to a later part—either Reason's speeches ("you cause wise folk to withdraw from me," Love claims), or, more likely, the misogynistic passages, for the God of Love immediately jumps from his invective against the *Rose* to a condemnation of the portrait of Criseyde. And the dreamer's penance—to spend the rest of his life writing of good women—is supposed to atone both for *Troilus and Criseyde* and the *Rose.* Thus, the God of Love's words suggest two important ideas. First, Chaucer almost certainly translated more than the 1,705 lines of the remaining fragment of the *Romaunt.* Second, the *Rose* was known in England as a misogynistic work about the same time that Christine de Pizan and allies were attacking it in France for the same reason.

In these three passages Chaucer suggests that for him the *Rose* is a monumental work, the greatest work on love, but there is a mocking tone in his exaggerations (the entire work and its gloss painted on the walls, the impossibility of describing a garden better than the *Rose* does). Chaucer's admiration for the *Rose* is real but playful. Furthermore, the prologue to the *Legend of Good Women* suggests the ambiguity of the art of love contained in the *Rose,* an art that includes both attacks on love that anger the god himself and passages that inspire Chaucer's most effective writings on love (as Queen Alceste, the God of Love's companion, ironically points out in his defense). The *Rose's* complex and conflicting views of love not only inspire Chaucer's early love poetry, for which he was well known in his own time, but continue to challenge him throughout his life.

There are a number of "levels of flow" from the *Rose* to Chaucer, from the most specific level of the similarities of certain lines, to the most general, that of a model for literary creation. Most scholars, until recently at least, have concentrated on the level of linguistic echoes. Some of the earliest examples of this approach came from French scholars, who, like Etienne Gustave Sandras, tried to show that England's greatest medieval poet was practically a French poet in disguise.[35] At the end of the nineteenth century English scholars continued to match lines from Chaucer's works with more or less similar ones in the *Rose*.[36] Then a reaction set in and scholars began to look for Chaucer's originality, his independence from the *Rose*, by rejecting many of the supposed similarities. Thus Cipriani and Fansler question many of the supposed allusions to the *Rose* in Chaucer's work, although they continue to assume that such correspondences can be found and that they are meaningful.[37]

Today scholars are rarely interested in line-for-line matching as a means of determining influence. The methodological problems involved in such an approach are so great that such a "match" proves very little. Similarities in tone or wording may result from a common ancestor (Boethius, for example, whom Chaucer and Jean de Meun had translated), or from an intermediary like Guillaume de Machaut. In any case, medieval borrowing from and adaptation of other works is so continuous that little is learned of Chaucer's debt to the *Rose* by counting corresponding lines; intertextuality (one work's response to, its playing off of, another work) was a fundamental literary principle in the Middle Ages.

More recently scholars have looked for broader areas of agreement in Chaucer's work and the *Rose*, such as characterization, adaptation of embedded narratives, or views of love (see Lynn King Morris's work, which lists studies of the *Rose*'s influence on Chaucer for a dozen of the early works and nineteen of the twenty-four *Canterbury Tales*).[38] Such an approach requires a more careful reading of the art and ideas of both poets.

Scholars often see Chaucer's early works as influenced by Guillaume de Lorris and the later works, especially the *Canterbury Tales*, as drawing on Jean de Meun, as if the diachronic narrative of the *Rose* paralleled the chronology of Chaucer's creativity. Is Guillaume de Lorris, therefore, a young man's poet, because he wrote of idealistic love, while Jean de Meun wrote for the disabused older man? This oversimplification of Chaucer has been challenged by James Wimsatt: "Particularly as reflected in Chaucer's work, the poems of Guillaume and Jean occupy common and contiguous, rather than opposing areas of the poetic sphere."[39] He goes on to point out "courtly" passages that can be traced to Jean and "realistic" ones to Guillaume. However, keeping in mind this continuous presence of both *Rose* poets in Chaucer's work, we can

see that the earlier works were more influenced by Guillaume's imaginary world than the later works.

Four of the early poems are set as dreams that contain many of the
elements of Guillaume's dream: the *Book of the Duchess,* the *Parliament
of Fowls,* the *House of Fame,* and the prologue to the *Legend of Good
Women.* Two of these works refer to "king Scipion" (*Book of the Duchess,*
286, and *House of Fame,* 916), a mistake that Chaucer picked up from
Guillaume de Lorris (Scipio was not royalty), one that suggests that his
knowledge of Macrobius's *Somnium Scipionis* came from the French poet,
not from the original (which he has read, however, by the time he
wrote the *Parliament of Fowls*). Chaucer's use of the dream frame varies
considerably in these poems; he is closest to Guillaume in the *Book of
the Duchess,* although even here he reworks the dream garden. Though
Chaucer takes many of the "appurtenances" of the dream from his
French sources, including Machaut, he is clearly more interested in the
dream as a means to create an otherworldly illusion.[40] For this purpose
Guillame's dream is the primary literary model.

Chaucer also shows both his reading of the *Rose* and his independence
from it in his use of personifications. Abstractions either occur as a
form of diction ("Trouthe hymself," for example, in the *Book of the
Duchess*), or they appear as static figures in a Renaissance-style tableau
in the *Parliament of Fowls,* figures that include Delyt, Beute, Youthe,
Gentilesse, and Desyr. But almost nowhere does Chaucer incorporate
his view of human interaction into personified abstractions. Instead he
expresses various views of love, folly, lust, and charity through indi-
vidualized characters. Troilus, for example, lives through many of the
Lover's experiences in the *Rose,* but not as a simple representation of
passionate love. (Although *Troilus and Criseyde* contains no personifications, Cipriani can claim that "the influence of the Romance of the
Rose on Chaucer shows itself more distinctly in the *Troylus* than in any
other single poem.")[41] Similarly, Pandarus is a more complex, more
human realization of the companion and confidant than Guillaume's
Friend. In a later work Chaucer even humanizes the ponderous Neoplatonic personification, Nature, through her wise, patient presiding
over the birds' debate on the nature of true love in the *Parliament of
Fowls.* And like Jean, Geoffrey leaves the final judgment open, thereby
drawing the audience into the debate.

This process of individualizing, of humanizing the characters of the
Rose continues in the satiric types from the continuation that Chaucer
chose to incorporate into the *Canterbury Tales.* The Pardoner and the

Wife of Bath both reflect their ancestors, False Seeming and the Old Woman, but they also stand alone as original creations (see discussion of the Old Woman above). The Pardoner reveals many of the same motivations as False Seeming: he covetously preaches against covetousness:

> Of avarice and of swich cuursednesse
> Is al my prechyng, for to make hem free
> To yeven hir pens, and namely unto me.[42]

(Of avarice and of such cursedness is all my preaching, to make them give freely of their pence, especially to me.)

He rejects poverty under the guise of holiness, and he uses his preaching to avenge himself on those who trespass against him or his brethren.[43] But we can see him in action more clearly than we can False Seeming, for he shows himself hawking his wonderful relics to his trusting public, like the charlatans of such medieval French plays as Rutebeuf's *Dit de l'Herberie*.

Chaucer borrowed more than satiric types from Jean: he learned from his predecessor the possibilities of dialogues like those between the Dreamer and the Black Knight in the *Book of the Duchess*; he adapted stories from Jean's work in "The Monk's Tale" and "The Physician's Tale" as well as many exempla and classical references in other tales. But there is more. As Wimsatt points out, Jean widened immensely the range of love poetry for later poets,[44] so that Chaucer saw the possibility of exploring the variety of human love experiences. Furthermore, in part because of his familiarity with the *Rose,* he learned to balance the idealistic and realistic styles that French poetry tended to separate, as Muscatine has argued in *Chaucer and the French Tradition*.

But there is still more. In one sense, it is clear that Chaucer would not have been the poet he was without the *Rose*. But we must go a step further than previous scholars, who see the influence of the *Rose* as providing Chaucer's poetry with narrative techniques, images, themes, "raw material." The importance of the *Rose* for Chaucer is that its existence, on the horizon of what poetry could do, challenged Chaucer to reach farther than he might otherwise have done, to ask questions about humankind that he might otherwise not have asked. The *Rose* is the highest peak that a late medieval poet confronted, and though many others (Machaut, Froissart, Gower) climbed part way, it was only Chaucer, through his genius, who was able to see the whole mountain, to see it and to go beyond to a new and original synthesis. The *Rose* contributed to Chaucer's greatness by stretching his poetic ambitions and strengthening his creative muscles, but without that inherent greatness he could not have responded to the *Rose* as he did. This is the most far-reaching influence that one poet can have on another.

Italy

Boccaccio, Dante, and Petrarch knew the *Rose,* as did many lesser Italian writers of the fourteenth and fifteenth centuries. Although we do not know how available manuscripts of the *Rose* were in this period, references to the work indicate that it was read in some circles at least (in Florence, for example), where it was thought of both as the highest achievement of French literature and as a link to classical Latin authors such as Ovid. Thus, according to Earl Jeffrey Richards, "not surprisingly, the earliest attempts at It[alian] narrative (*Tesoretto, Fiore, Intelligenza*) all show the influence of the *Rose.*"[45] The *Rose* became known in Italy at a crucial time in the development of an Italian vernacular literature, for in the thirteenth century poets were deeply concerned with the possibility of achieving in their own language what had been done in Latin, Provençal, and French. For these poets, including Dante, the *Rose* was a model of extended verse narration in the vernacular.

The first works in Italian that adapt or borrow from the *Rose* were often generically innovative. Brunetto Latini, for example, introduced elements from the *Rose* into his Italian adaptation in verse, the *Tesoretto,* of his earlier work, *Li Livres dou Trésor* (The book of the treasure), a prose *summa* written in French at the end of the thirteenth century. Latini's *Tesoretto* (Little treasure) borrows from the *Rose* "the use of narrator-protagonist, the poeticization of philosophical discourse and cosmology and the *bel prato.*"[46] Latini recognized the way the *Rose* dealt poetically with philosophical questions and used this insight to "poeticize" his own philosophical treatise.

Another work from this period is even more experimental: the *Fiore* attempts to translate the *Rose* into a cycle of 232 sonnets, which transpose both the narrative and lyrical elements of the *Rose* while omitting some of the philosophical discussions of the second part. Of debated authorship, a number of scholars have argued that the *Fiore* was probably composed by Dante himself.[47] If this were true, what place would the *Fiore* occupy in the development of Dante's work? Recognizing the monumental differences between the *Fiore* and the *Divine Comedy*, scholars have viewed the sonnet cycle as a youthful work that Dante later turned away from, and the *Divine Comedy* has been described therefore as a palinode or "anti-parody" of the *Fiore*.[48] If current scholarly opinion questions Dante's authorship, it is nonetheless likely that Dante knew well the *Fiore*. Certain gallicisms, for example, occur only in the *Fiore* and the *Divine Comedy*.[49] The *Rose* may therefore have influenced Dante's conception of love indirectly, through this unusual translation.

But when did Dante become familiar with the *Rose* itself? A fourteenth-century French writer, Laurent de Premierfait, claimed that Dante was inspired by the *Rose* to compose the *Divine Comedy*.[50] This chauvinistic claim has never been proved. It appears probable that Dante had read the *Rose* before writing *Paradiso,* but if he had read it, and even translated it, in his formative years (about 1285), we would expect to see evidence of this knowledge in earlier works, specifically in Dante's discussion of French literature in his *De vulgari eloquentia* (written 1304). Yet the only reference to French writing there is to prose (chap. 1, part 10, section 2). We would also expect to see allusions to the *Rose* in the *Divine Comedy,* but few reminiscences have been shown to exist before the end of *Purgatorio.*

John Took and Earl Jeffrey Richards represent the two extreme positions in the question of the influence of the *Rose* on Dante: Took offers a hodge-podge of possible reminiscences in the *Vita nuova,* the *Convivio,* and the *Divine Comedy,*[51] while Richards cautiously suggests five possible passages from the end of the *Divine Comedy* for comparison with similar passages in the *Rose*. These passages include the Earthly Paradise (*Purgatorio,* cantos 27–30), which suggests elements of Love's Garden in the *Rose*; Beatrice's discourse on moonspots (*Paradiso,* canto 2) and Nature's remarks on moonspots; and the river of light, fountain of light and celestial Rose (*Paradiso,* canto 33) and the *fontaine de vie* in the Park of the Good Shepherd.[52]

The *Dictionary of the Middle Ages* summarizes the question of the *Rose*'s influence cautiously: "It seems altogether possible that he became aware of the French work only late in his life, that it was an important rival and analogue in the *Paradiso,* and that he was not the author of the *Fiore.* The whole question, like so many concerning Dante, is in need of further study."[53] Yet, although we cannot determine when

Dante became familiar with the *Rose,* Richards argues persuasively that the principal consequence of the familiarity was a profound one: Dante was made aware, through the *Rose,* of the possibility of creating in his own language what had been done in its great predecessor, Latin.

Scholars refer to the medieval writer's attitude toward his predecessors as the *translatio* theme, the belief that a contemporary literary work continues an earlier work by adapting it to the author's own purposes. "From this perspective, the authenticity (and concomitant truthfulness) of a poetic text derive from its conjoining of inherited poetic tradition and contemporary poetic experience."[54] As Jean de Meun described his work, in the midpoint of the *Rose,* as the continuation not only of Guillaume de Lorris but of the great Latin writers on love such as Ovid, Richards argues that Dante also saw his poem as a re-creation of the great works of his Latin predecessors (see *Inferno,* 4. 100–103). Thus, though it is probably incorrect to say that the *Rose* was the inspiration for the *Divine Comedy,* it is probably true that the *Rose* aided Dante's understanding of vernacular narrative's potential to unite philosophy and poetry. Ultimately, this is the greatest influence that the *Rose* had not only on Dante but on European literature as a whole.

Chapter Five
Critical History of the *Roman de la rose*

The *Rose* was the subject of the earliest critical debate in French literature, as we saw in the "Querelle de la Rose." Scholars and writers in France found the *Rose* of critical interest until about the middle of the sixteenth century, after which it was little read until the middle of the eighteenth. Since about 1850, critical interest in the *Rose* has grown, but because of its inherent complexity and ambiguity there remains little agreement on some major questions of interpretation, In this chapter we will review the critical history of the *Rose* from the Renaissance to the present. Criticism before Ernest Langlois's edition (1914–24) will be presented chronologically, after Langlois, in terms of the principal critical questions that have concerned scholars.

Early Criticism of the *Rose*

The *Rose* was widely printed and, evidently, still widely read at the end of the fifteenth century and the first half of the sixteenth, for twenty-one editions were printed from 1480 to 1538. The fifteenth-century poet Jean Molinet claimed that the *Rose* had become incorporated into human memory, that its important sentences had become "proverbes communs." If it was read, however, it was no longer easy reading; the average educated reader of the time was having difficulty both with the work's language and its allegory. This state of affairs lead two poets in this period, Molinet and Clement Marot, to publish editions designed to make the *Rose* more comprehensible to their contemporaries.

Molinet produced a prose version of the *Rose,* entitled *Le Romant de la rose moralisié cler et net* (*The Romance of the rose,* moralized clear and proper), published in 1500, although written somewhat earlier. His "moralization" of the *Rose,* which gives every detail a pious interpretation, imposes on the *Rose* an allegorization that destroys both the

meaning and intent of the original. For example, the Lover's approach
to the river, at the beginning of the dream, is interpreted as the infant
delivered from its mother's womb and washed in the holy baptismal
font. Although such outrageous distortions may make modern readers
smile, there are scholars today who appear to be following the principle
that Molinet states in his prologue, that of converting "le corporel en
spirituel, la mondanité en divinité" (the corporal to the spiritual, the
worldly to the divine).[1] Despite the skillful analyses of scholars like
Rosemund Tuve,[2] there are still no accepted criteria for distinguishing
"imposed allegory" from that which is consistent with the spirit of the
text.

In 1526 another and better poet, Clement Marot, published a modernized verse edition of the *Rose,* which he prefaced with his own view
of the moral allegory of the work. He, like Molinet, describes the high
esteem in which the *Rose* is held: "tant a esté de tous gens d'esprit
estimé que bien la daigne chascun veoir et tenir au plus hault anglet
de sa librairie pour les bonnes sentences, propos, et ditz naturelz et
moraulx qui dedans sont mis et inserez" (that is, cultured people are
proud to put the *Rose* in the place of honor in their libraries).[3] But
since some fear that the "fol amour" depicted in the work may corrupt
unwary readers, Marot suggests a possible interpretation of the work
that he hopes will make the author's good intentions clear, intentions
that are hidden under the "escorce" (bark) of the text.

Thus Marot, like Molinet, imposes on the text a pious interpretation. He specifically offers not just one, but many, allegorizations of
the Rose: it represents wisdom, the state of grace, the glorious Virgin
Mary, and, finally, eternal bliss. Like many later readers, Marot feels
that his admiration for the beautiful fable is threatened by its apparent
immorality, which he then explains in a way that allows the work to
keep its place in his admiration. Both Marot and Molinet think of the
Rose as a beloved friend with some unfortunate moral traits, who can
be redeemed through a reinterpretation of those traits.

The *Rose* continued to be admired by poets and scholars for the first
half of the sixteenth century. Ronsard, the greatest poet of the period,
recommended it as one of the few medieval works still worth reading,
and in his youth he wrote a curious little meditation on the *Rose.*[4] An
outstanding humanist scholar, Etienne Pasquier, compared it favorably
to the *Divine Comedy* (see *L,* 1:37–38). Then for two hundred years it
was mentioned only by a few writers, like the seventeenth-century nov-
elist Charles Sorel in his *Bibliothèque françoise.*

The eighteenth century has long been considered strongly critical of the Middle Ages (it was then that the term "gothic" began to be used derogatorily). An indication that this is an oversimplification is the fact that the Enlightenment also saw the first new edition of the *Rose* after a silence of two hundred years.[5] In 1735 Lenglet du Fresnoy published an edition that he preceded with the first philological and literary study of the *Rose*. At least four other editions were projected in the eighteenth century, and several studies, largely historical or moral, were printed.[6] Clearly the *Rose* was again finding an audience. In his preface Lenglet du Fresnoy reaffirms the importance of the *Rose* in French literary history ("our Homer," he calls it), discusses its date and its view of love (while rebuking the Lover for heartlessly abandoning his mistress), and analyzes the moral content and literary structure. This edition was reprinted for almost a century.

The Méon edition of the *Rose* in 1814 was, according to Michel Defourny, "la première véritable édition critique" (the first true critical edition), the first to be based on manuscripts rather than incunabula.[7] In addition to the text of the romance, Méon reprinted a number of earlier studies, including Lenglet du Fresnoy's introduction, and he added several works attributed to Jean de Meun, the *Codicile* and the *Testament*. Thus this edition made available to interested readers a fairly reliable text of the *Rose* and the major critical studies of it.[8] During the course of the century it was reprinted several times by others, with some variants (mostly unfortunate).

It is therefore surprising that there were no important critical studies of the *Rose* until the end of the nineteenth century, a century in which interest in medieval literature was strong. The critical discussions of the *Rose* appeared mainly in journal articles and histories of French literature and were largely summaries and cursory attempts to situate the work in the history of medieval literature. At the end of the century, however, scholars began to look more closely at the *Rose*. The great medievalist, Gaston Paris, gave twelve pages to the *Rose* in his literary survey, *La littérature française au Moyen Age*.[9] Although he recognized the originality of Guillaume's personifications, he faulted this allegorical approach for its artificiality, which, he felt, relieved the author of the need for realistic observation of emotions, and he argued that Guillaume's imitators pushed this fault to excess. But Paris recognized the skillful construction of Guillaume's allegory and the elegance of his style.

Paris treats Jean de Meun, however, to even more severe criticism:

his work is described as a kind of shapeless monster, a hodge-podge of everything that Jean thought and knew. (Gaston Paris's father, Paulin Paris, had expressed a similar idea thirty years earlier when he argued that Jean used Guillaume's story to express his own broad scientific knowledge.)[10] Yet Gaston Paris evidently admired Jean de Meun, for he called him "le Voltaire du moyen âge."[11] For many years scholars accepted Gaston Paris's views of the essential characteristics of the two parts of the *Rose,* that Guillaume's allegory was elegant but artificial, while Jean was only interested in the philosophical digressions that he could insert into the love story.

Then came Langlois. Ernest Langlois's lifelong study of the *Rose* produced three monumental works, the foundation of modern scholarship on the *Rose.* In 1891 he published *Les origines and sources du "Roman de la Rose,"* in 1910 his study of the manuscripts, and from 1914 to 1924 his five-volume edition. These works are interrelated, for the first two were undertaken as preparation for the third.

In *Origines* and the first volume of the edition, Langlois reiterates the view that the two parts of the *Rose* are fundamentally opposed, that Guillaume's part is characterized by grace and finesse, "mesure et tact," Jean's by a "caractère encyclopédique," that is, one is characterized by sensitivity, the other by intelligence (an opposition that will be repeated by many later critics). In fact, Jean loses sight of the subject of the work because he is interested only in educating his readers.[12] The explanation for the differences in the two parts, Langlois believes, lies in the differences in the publics for which they were written, one noble, the other bourgeois.

Furthermore, Langlois argues that Jean had no definite plan in mind while he was writing the *Rose.*[13] This is perhaps the most extreme statement of the view, held by many scholars, that Jean's continuation has no organization, no structure, that he was only interested in producing a series of discourses on various topics that constitute so many digressions from the narrative. More recently, scholars have adopted the hypothesis that Jean did have definite literary goals and that his method of composition followed accepted medieval principles. One of the major tasks that scholars such as Alan Gunn (in *The Mirror of Love*) have set themselves is to better understand these principles and to place the so-called digressions into a context that reveals their essential connection to the work as a whole.

Many of the ideas that Langlois expressed in *Origines* were also expressed in Gustave Lanson's influential study of the *Rose* that appeared three years later.[14] Lanson also argued that the two parts of the *Rose* were written by absolutely incompatible thinkers, that Jean's enclyclopedic continuation is a disordered compilation of a variety of topics, that Jean was "un vrai bourgeois." It is surprising to learn that Jean's supposed misogyny is "une des plus authentiques marques de bourgeoisie dans une oeuvre litteraire" (one of the most authentic signs of the middle class in a literary work).[15]

Lanson was one of the first, however, to attempt to see a unifying philosophy in Jean's continuation, which he calls "un sérieux et solide naturalisme" (a serious and solid naturalism), "un système complet de philosophie" (a complete philosophical system) already liberated from theology.[16] Jean, according to Lanson, argued that the fundamental law of human life is to follow Nature, that is, to procreate. This naturalism underlies Jean's ideas on such subjects as social classes and the monastic orders. But Jean was also a Christian and consequently saw the necessary relation of Nature to Reason, "the unity and sovereignty of Nature and Reason." Thus Lanson sees no contradiction between Reason's point of view and Nature's—the command to procreate goes hand in hand with the Christian virtues that Reason prescribes.

This remarkable article, which attempted to give Jean de Meun the place he deserves in French literature, had a decisive influence on criticism of the *Rose* for many years. Although many of Lanson's views have since been modified or abandoned, the question of Jean's conception of Nature, and of man's nature, is one that continues to challenge critical thinking.

Modern Critical Approaches

Modern criticism of the *Rose* has been above all a quest for meaning. The meaning of individual elements—the Rose, the Fountain of Narcissus, Reason, and the other major personifications—but also the meaning of the work as a whole and of each of the parts. Except for those who have assumed that Guillaume de Lorris was simply writing about love, or that Jean de Meun was simply showing off his learning, most critics have proceeded on the belief that this most complex allegorical work does have several levels of meaning.

In the past fifty years the questions posed, and the critical assumptions presupposed, in this quest for meaning have formed a dialogue that reflects the evolution of modern critical approaches to the *Rose*. Because of lack of space, this chapter cannot discuss all the studies written on the *Rose* in the past fifty years. Instead of a chronological survey of *Rose* scholarship, therefore, I will analyze the kinds of questions that critics have asked of the *Rose,* questions based on implicit assumptions about the nature of the work. This approach allows students of the *Rose* to place the critical works they read in the context of the principal critical hypotheses concerning it. [17]

Critics have asked three major questions about Guillaume de Lorris's *Rose*: What is the nature of the love that he describes? Has he or has he not given us the deeper meaning to which he alludes? Did he or did he not finish the work? Many studies do not appear to address these questions directly but attempt instead to describe Guillaume's allegorical method. However, an author's approach to Guillaume's allegory reflects, as we shall see, implicit answers to these three questions.

Guillaume's Lover appears to be an ideal representative of thirteenth-century courtly society. In the beginning he has the necessary potential to become the perfect vassal of the God of Love, but he must first go through a difficult initiation during which he learns to make his passion, and his behavior, conform to courtly values. Thus it has frequently been argued, especially by French scholars, that the "vices" banned from the garden, the "virtues" represented by Lord Merriment and friends, the rules laid down by the God of Love, the Lover's sufferings, all reflect the ideals of the French nobility in Guillaume's time. [18]

Even this most explicit level of meaning has provoked critical disagreement. As we saw in chapter 2, the critical usefulness of the term "courtly love" has been seriously questioned in the past twenty years. For those scholars who reject the term, and therefore the idea that the Middle Ages invented a new kind of love, Guillaume's Lover is simply suffering from adulterous passion. But even among the critics who accept the term as a useful way to refer to the system of values and feelings expressed in certain medieval works intended for a courtly audience, there are those who see courtly love primarily as a psychological phenomenon, others who approach it as an expression of social forces, still others who describe it as a set of generic constraints and who see courtly literature as a kind of intricate literary game. These three realities are of course interrelated, and each has been the subject of critical studies that approach the *Rose* as an allegory of courtly love.

The characteristics that critics have traditionally attributed to courtly literature as a genre are those that they also attribute to the first part of the *Rose*—delicacy, subtlety, discreet suggestion rather than didacticism, sentimentality. Guillaume's work has consequently been seen as the epitome of French courtly literature (or is it that the first part of the *Rose* has been taken as the typical courtly work from which the characteristics of the genre are derived?). But a scholar must decide, when describing Guillaume's portrayal of courtly values, whether the poet admiringly accepted those values or ironically questioned their validity. Irony, though, which is often the result of tone or suggestion, is a difficult matter for scholars to agree on.[19]

Many approaches to the first part of the *Rose* see the courtly context as the narrative covering for a noncourtly allegorical meaning. For D. W. Robertson, John V. Fleming, and others, courtly love is the signifier, Man's Fall from grace the signified. This hypothesis leads to the reinterpretation of many essential elements of the *Rose,* such as the Fountain of Narcissus, personifications like Oisive (Idleness), and above all the Lover's rejection of Reason. It also requires the inversion of the apparent values of the *Rose*—Jealousy and friends become "good guys" (redemptive elements), and the Lover, the God of Love, and their allies become villains. Such a feat of interpretation is achieved in part by putting much of the romance into the ironic mode. Since this interpretation argues that the allegory of the Fall and of the nature of sin continues in Jean de Meun's part, I will discuss there the advantages and difficulties of this view of the *Rose.*

Guillaume promises several times to explain in the end the meaning of his allegory of love. Scholars generally assume that he did not give us his meaning because he did not finish his romance. Both of these assumptions have been questioned. Some have argued that it is the God of Love's lecture to the Lover that constitutes Guillaume's meaning; the God of Love is his glosser, his interpreter. Most scholars, however, believe that the deeper meaning of the work (if there is one, if Guillaume was not simply playing with our expectations) has not been given to us by the work itself and that we must find it through our interpretation of the work as a whole.

Whether we see the work as unfinished, as Jean himself argued, or essentially finished, this assumption influences our interpretation of its meaning. Scholars have taken three positions regarding the end of the work: it is finished; it is nearly finished; it is unfinished. If Guillaume's *Rose* is complete, it is a work in the lyric mode, like the courtly chanson and is essentially a tragic view of love's sufferings. If it is incomplete, Guillaume intended to unite the Lover with his Rose (although certainly not as Jean de Meun did it) and therefore the *Rose* is a more optimistic narrative, in the romance tradition (see chapter 3 above). This second view of the ending supports the interpretation of the *Rose* as a bildungsroman, the story of a young man's maturing through the experience of a great passion. And this interpretation brings us back to the first question we asked of Guillaume, the significance of the Lover's quest for the Rose.

Scholars have not focused their attention equally on both parts of the *Rose,* for from the beginning readers have shown a preference for one part or the other. Until the twentieth century Guillaume's *Rose* was generally preferred, although even those who greatly favored Guillaume were awed by Jean's 18,000-line continuation. In any case, few readers have stayed unmoved—either by admiration or scorn—by the second part. In general critical attention has shifted to Jean's part since the nadir, C. S. Lewis's condemnation of Jean's "huge, dishevelled, violent poem";[20] in the past fifty years more studies have been written on Jean's *Rose* than on Guillaume's, and those critical works that discuss the entire romance generally are more interested in the second part.[21]

This is not simply a reflection of the fact that there is more material for scrutiny in the continuation. I believe that, if the first part is seen as a tour de force of taste and sentiment, and the second as a remarkable intellectual construction, this shift in modern critical favor may reflect the shift from an interest in the portrayal of psychological states to a concern for the artistic manipulation of ideas and language.

The major critical questions asked of the second part of the *Rose* have been: Is there an underlying philosophy? If so, how is it expressed? And how does the continuation relate to Guillaume's poem? The most basic question that a reader faces in Jean's *Rose* is whether he had a reason, other than pedantry, for everything he wrote. Did Jean have an underlying philosophy? C. S. Lewis, again, gave the most adamant "no": "Jean de Meun has no final view either of love or of anything else."[22] Alan Gunn, at the other extreme, has argued that everything, or nearly everything, in the second part is linked to Jean's view of love: "neither in the portion composed by Guillaume de Lorris nor in that composed by Jean de Meun is there any extended digression from the general subject of love."[23] Even passages apparently remote from this subject, such as those on alchemy and optics, are shown by Gunn to be intimately related to it.[24]

Between these two positions we find scholars who recognize the existence of digressions in the second part but who argue that a unifying philosophy is nonetheless present (in the nondigressive parts). The nature of this philosophy, and the critical method adopted to find evidence for it, are the major problems facing *Rose* scholars.

The critical search for Jean's message has concentrated on the speeches of the principal personifications rather than on the narrative itself. The assumption underlying this approach is that one or more characters speak for the author himself. The problem is to determine which one. No scholar, as far as I know, has discussed the basis on which he or she chose to accept the words of a particular character as also those of Jean de Meun. Unfortunately, Jean nowhere indicates explicitly whom we are to believe.

Before the arrival of D. W. Robertson's patristic theory, most scholars looked for the *Rose*'s message in Nature and Genius; after Robertson, French writers still favor these characters, while many English-speaking critics emphasize the weight of tradition behind Reason's arguments. This is why we find such astonishingly contradictory summations of the *Rose* as these: "Jean de Meun's poem is a warning to heed the voice of reason, and to avoid desire that may lead to hypocritical behavior and adultery in the heart";[25] "Par delà l'aventure individuelle du songeur amant, ce qui est espéré dans le texte est le triomphe universel et définitif de l'Eros" (Beyond the individual adventure of the lover-dreamer, what is hoped for in the text is the universal and definitive triumph of Eros).[26] Both scholars believe that the *Rose* is talking about desire, but they are far apart in their view of what it is saying.

The choice of an authoritative voice in the *Rose* can be made in one of three ways. Many scholars take up one character, such as Reason, as the author's representative. Others take up several (usually Nature and Genius, although Nature and Reason are sometimes made bedfellows). Still others choose passages from all the characters, ignoring thereby the principle of decorum (discussed above, chapter 4). Even lines attributed to a speaker within a character's speech have been cited as the opinion of the author himself. Thus Gustave Cohen affirms that "our author" approves Jupiter's words, spoken by Genius: "Pleasure, as Jupiter used to say, is the supreme good in life" (ll. 20075–77).[27] It is surprising to see attributed to Jean de Meun the opinions of the scoundrel Jupiter, who castrated his father, Saturn, and ended the Golden Age of mankind.

Quoting from various characters is a common approach in *Rose* criticism, since it is tempting to pull out the many concise, catchy phrases which seem to focus on an idea important to the author. "Trop est fort chose que Nature, / el passe neïs nourreture" (ll. 14007–8; Nature is a very powerful thing, it surpasses even upbringing); "Ainsinc va des contreres choses, / les unes sunt des autres gloses" (ll. 21543–44; Thus it is with contrary things, one kind explains the other); "Car soffisance fet richece" (l. 18535; Sufficiency makes wealth). Lines such as these are often cited without regard to context, on the assumption that it does not matter that the first was said by the Old Woman, the second by the Lover, the third by Nature. The fundamental problem with this approach is that it supposes that Jean has not taken into account the nature of a certain character when he has him or her speak a certain way, that what the Old Woman or the Friend or Genius says may be as valid as the words of Reason or Nature. By obviating the fictional basis of Jean's creation, this approach turns the characters into transparent mediums for the author's "message."

Many scholars who focus on one or more characters as the principal authority do not discuss what the others are there for; they even ignore apparent oppositions, such as that between Reason and Nature. They seem to view the *Rose* as an expression of the medieval theory of the "two truths," that contradictory positions may both be true in their own realms. Nature, for example, may speak for this contingent, changing world, while Reason is seen as expressing immutable, spiritual truths. If scholars allude to characters other than the author's spokesmen, it is usually assumed that they are traditional satiric or didactic characters and therefore not central to Jean's world view. Few scholars have attempted to formulate an interpretation that synthesizes all the major personifications, perhaps because of the complexity and scope of the arguments in the second part, or perhaps because the opposition between the authorities is irreducible. (I will return to this subject in the last chapter.)

The first major theory about Jean's message was called naturalism, and it privileged the character Nature. The studies of Marcel Françon, Helmut Hatzfeld, F. W. Müller, Gérard Paré, Alan Gunn, and others argue that Jean's thought was a form of naturalism.[28] They point to Jean's evident admiration for the beauty and order of the natural world, for his supposed belief that natural law is the highest value in human life (in this world). Françon, for example, states succinctly the central idea of the second part of the *Roman de la rose*: "c'est que la Nature est souveraine et que l'homme n'a rien de mieux à faire que d'obéir à ses commandements" (that Nature is sovereign and . . . that man can do nothing better than obey her commands).[29] Despite the emphasis on the importance of Nature in the *Rose,* there are of course differences in the points of view of these scholars, especially concerning the Christian or pagan orientation of Jean's naturalism.

Furthermore, natural law is seen as the basis for Jean's critique of society, especially his remarks about true nobility, the Golden Age, and the Mendicant Orders. Even Reason becomes, according to this hypothesis, a subsidiary of Nature's laws (does not Reason recognize the value of procreation in God's scheme?). Each of the *Rose's* characters is judged, therefore, by how closely he or she follows the true law of nature, which may be seen as simply the need to procreate or more generally as the laws by which the individual reaches its fullest development (the personification of Nature was discussed more fully in chapter 3). Gunn gives the broadest interpretation of Jean's naturalism by connecting it to the "philosophy of plenitude," the belief that through God's goodness "the entire universe is filled with a continuous chain of being from the highest to the lowest."[30]

One of the consequences of this interpretation is that it has led scholars to investigate the intellectual influences on Jean de Meun, from the works of his predecessors, Alain de Lille and other twelfth-century Platonists, to the heterodox Aristotelians such as Siger de Brabant who were Jean's contemporaries. These studies have shown to what extent Jean's ideas about nature were shaped by other thinkers. Since some of these ideas appear to conflict with orthodox Christian thinking, especially the idea of the value of procreation, scholars have been concerned to determine whether Jean had strayed from orthodox teachings about Nature, how far he had gone toward heresy.

The interpretation developed by Gérard Paré exemplifies both the strengths and weaknesses of the theory of naturalism. Paré argues that the central idea of Jean de Meun's conception of love is found in Nature's "law" that the good of the species is the only legitimate goal of love.[31] All the other personifications also urge this view, in their own ways. This "doctrine de l'amour" is expressed most bluntly, according to Paré, in Genius's sermon. While this interpretation has the merit of recognizing the importance of Nature in Jean's thought and of attempting to place that thought in the intellectual context of Paris in the late thirteenth century, it also has some serious drawbacks.

This theory of naturalism leads Paré to posit a disturbing contradiction in Jean's thinking: his theories of nature and society are traditional, even orthodox (and not naturalistic, because Jean makes nature subordinate to God), while his theories of love and sex are not only naturalistic but heterodox, even heretical.[32] Although Paré does not explain this bizarre opposition, it still needs to be examined. It is not sufficient to point out that the ideas of Nature and Genius are similar to those attributed to the "heterodox Aristotelians," ideas condemned in 1277. Jean viewed ironically Genius's claim that procreation was, in Paré's words, "a foretaste and sign of paradise."[33] It is significant that no medieval writer links Jean and the heterodox Aristotelians, though several object to what they see as Jean's excessive attention to Venus.

Paré is of course not the only scholar to have observed apparent contradictions in Jean's "philosophy." Others have devised ingenious but paradoxical labels in their attempts to grasp both ends of the stick, labels such as "Christian phallicism" (Gunn) and "courtly scholasticism" (Gorce). The problem of the limits and meaning of Jean's naturalism is still with us.

The answers to these difficult questions are important for our understanding of the originality of Jean's thought. Some scholars consider his view of nature as a reworking of traditional thought, while others see him as a precursor of such revolutionary social thinkers as Voltaire and Rousseau.[34] For Jean's theory of nature is the counterpart of his theory of the basis of contemporary society and of the characteristics of the ideal society. Nature and society, topics that come up over and over in the *Rose,* are clearly central concerns of the author, regardless of how we understand his thinking about them. Therefore, a number of scholars, especially in France, have attempted to bring together into a coherent system the remarks about society scattered through the *Rose.* These remarks sometimes lead to a view of Jean as an original social thinker, one with almost modern ideas about social equality.[35]

The third major hypothesis concerning the meaning of the *Rose,* one that uses the exegetical method in order to reach an orthodox Christian interpretation, was first proposed by D. W. Robertson. This much-debated theory interprets the *Rose* as an allegory both of Man's Fall from Grace and of the process inherent in any act of sinning, but especially that of lust. Thus the second part of the romance continues the story begun by Guillaume of the consequences of the lustful Lover's rejection of Reason. The advocates of this theory have concentrated on showing how Reason expresses traditional patristic thinking and how the other characters all have wrong-headed ideas about love. The *Rose* is placed in the context not of medieval secular philosophy (Neoplatonism and Aristotelianism) but of the writings of the church fathers.

It is true, as the Robertsonians argue, that we need to understand medieval religious thinking in order to understand medieval literature, that literary works cannot be divorced from their cultural context (if we do not forget that the relation of intellectual history to literary text is not a causal one). And although this theory has not been widely accepted, it does scholarship a service by raising some fundamental questions, for underlying this interpretation are major assumptions about medieval literature.

The first and most complex assumption concerns medieval culture. Robertson, Fleming, and Dahlberg assume that religious beliefs in the period of the *Rose* were largely homogeneous, that a medieval work as widely read as the *Rose* necessarily accepted the ideas of the church fathers. Fleming, for example, states categorically that he "cannot conceive of a convincing interpretation of the most popular poetic work of late medieval Christendom which will not be 'Christian'" (preface to *Roman de la rose*). This apparently simple statement incorporates several ambiguities. Fleming is playing on the word "Christian" in the large sense, implying that there was a single, common medieval religious mentality. (But is *Tristan et Iseult* a Christian work in the same way as *La Queste del Saint Graal?*). This assumption has been challenged, however, by scholars who point out that the thirteenth century saw such diverse thinkers as Saint Bonaventure and Siger de Brabant (see William Calin's remarks in his article, "Defense and Illustration").

Second, the term "popular" is misleading. Can we really use medieval "reader response" to the *Rose* as an indication of what Jean intended it to mean? There are a number of problems with this assumption. Pierre-Yves Badel has shown that readers responded to the *Rose* in a variety of ways, mostly for its satiric passages, rarely for a possible Christian message. Furthermore, if this message were as transparent to medieval readers as Robertson and Fleming claim, how do we explain the condemnation of the *Rose* by respected Christians like Jean Gerson, chancellor of the University of Paris, or the later Jean Molinet, who saw the need to moralize it? The argument from popularity simply does not work: many popular works in the Middle Ages do not support an Augustinian, or even a Christian interpretation—Chrétien de Troyes's *Lancelot,* for example, in which a lover also rejects reason in order to follow his passion, is not an allegory of the Fall. Finally we cannot assume that medieval readers applied the principles of biblical exegesis

(the four levels of allegory) to nonreligious works, since even the treatises on rhetoric do not generally recognize such a use of exegesis.

But Fleming goes well beyond arguing that the *Rose* is a "Christian"
work. He also contends that Jean's character Reason expresses Boethian
and Augustinian thinking, and that this personification is the key to
the allegory of the *Rose*. This is the strongest argument for interpreting
the *Rose* as a Christian allegory, if it could indeed be shown that Jean's
Reason is Augustinian.[36] Even if this were true, however, must we
conclude that no popular writer could have questioned the Augustinian
tradition? Must we assume, as Fleming seems to do, that if Jean created an Augustinian personification he must have accepted this personification as a satisfactory guide to one of life's most perplexing
experiences, sexual love? Jean undoubtedly accepted many Boethian
and Augustinian ideas (he translated Boethius, though some years after
the *Rose*), but he was also living during a time of intellectual turmoil
and change, a period that saw much debate on the question of the place
of sexuality in Christian life, of the value of chastity over procreation.
Therefore, although Reason in the *Rose* may represent patristic thinking, the Robertsonians have not shown that Jean necessarily found Au-
gustine the unquestioned moral guide to the problems of his world.

There is textual evidence that he did not. If, as Robertson and Fleming argue, the *Rose* portrays the consequences of the Lover's sinful rejection of Reason in favor of the God of Love, then Jean was a very
poor allegorist. Unlike the sinners of other medieval didactic works
(like the thirteenth-century play about a sinner, *Cortois d'Arras*), the
Lover suffers no adverse consequences for his behavior; in fact, he
achieves, happily, everything he set out to achieve. He triumphs, in
his own terms. Is it not significant that there is no palinode, no recan-
tation of the errors of one's ways, as in other didactic works? This is
poor pedagogy—to say one thing but do another—even if we are supposed to believe that Jean's view of the Lover is ironic. He does not
have his sinner even recognize his fault, much less show regret or do
penance. Is there a double message in the *Rose,* one from the supposed
allegorical meaning, the other from the narrative itself? And how are
we to explain the medieval popularity of this double-edged work, in
which an "increasingly stupid" hero (Fleming's words) blithely goes his
way unscathed? These are some of the questions raised by the assumptions at the base of the Robertsonian interpretation.

One of the methods employed to argue this approach also rests on a number of important assumptions. Evidence drawn from iconography is the major interpretative tool used by Fleming and others to determine a supposedly medieval reading (again a monolithic concept) of the *Rose*. (All other interpretations except theirs, they argue, are not medieval.)[37] The difficulty with this approach is that essential work is just now being done on the way the illuminators worked. Fleming and Dahlberg appear to assume that an illuminator had carefully read and formed an interpretation of the text before composing the miniature. The evidence seems to be rather that certain standard gestures and positions were used over and over.[38] It is at least possible that the position of the dreamer in the opening miniature of many *Rose* manuscripts resembles that of Mary at the Nativity because illuminators had drawn many more Marys than they had poets dreaming, and they adapted what they knew. Therefore, the iconographic approach to the meaning of the *Rose* must be used cautiously.

The Robertsonian interpretation argues that both parts of the *Rose* express a single allegorical meaning, that of sin and its consequences. In Fleming's words, "their poem prosecutes a single and unified action."[39] This raises the last critical question that I want to discuss, that of the unity or opposition of the two parts. Already in the Middle Ages a number of writers referred to what they saw as the differences between the two parts of the *Rose,* writers who included Christine de Pizan and Jean Gerson in the "Querelle de la Rose," Gui de Mori (who did an adaptation of the *Rose*), and the *Echecs amoureux* Commentator.[40] Since then scholars have continued to take positions regarding the unity of the *Rose,* with most seeing greater or lesser differences between the points of view of the work's two authors.

The recurring question is: Was Jean simply taking a different approach to the subject of love from that of his predecessor, or was he actively combatting Guillaume's views? Some scholars take a moderate position by claiming that Jean took up the frame provided by Guillaume in order to express his own philosophical concerns; the first part of the *Rose* was a pretext for the second.[41] Gunn argues that the subject of both parts is love: "there is no part which is not related in some way to the theme of love as variously interpreted by the different speakers."[42] He further believes that Jean was not hostile to Guillaume's view of courtly love, but he wanted to investigate all the other forms of human affection, including friendship, love of humanity, and sexual love. He points out that Guillaume describes his poem as an "art of love," that is, a didactic exposé of the proper behavior of a courtly lover, while Jean sees his work as a "mirror of love," an analysis of all the varieties of human love.[43]

This difference in purpose in the two parts is often attributed to the different social backgrounds of the respective authors, one noble, the other bourgeois. Because of his bourgeois background, Jean was unable to understand Guillaume's delicate allegory and subtle, suggestive style; Jean's views were necessarily more realistic, his style heavy and direct. This explanation was already popular with nineteenth-century scholars (see, for example, L, 1:25) and is still repeated today, although it is an unfortunate oversimplification of medieval cultural and intellectual history.

For most scholars, Jean took up Guillaume's story because he opposed its view of love; Jean was, in the words of Edmond Faral, "un anti-Guillaume de Lorris."[44] Paré called the second part of the *Rose* a "demolition" of the first, "une composition systématiquement ordonnée à ridiculiser les théories de l'amour courtois" (a composition systematically structured to ridicule the theories of courtly love).[45] It is often Genius's comparison of the Park of the Good Shepherd with Guillaume's Garden that is seen as the basis for this opposition, as though, again, Genius were speaking for his author. In the same way the misogynistic speeches of the second part are deemed to be a concerted attack on Guillaume's courtly view of love.

Although Jean's God of Love speaks of Jean as continuing Guillaume's work, there are both monumental and subtle differences between the two poems.[46] As we come to understand both parts of the *Rose* more clearly, we also see more clearly their differences, which concern both style and views of love. In the next chapter I will discuss some of these differences, especially the most fundamental one, the difference in the way the two poets see the relation of poetry to truth.

Chapter Six

Conclusion: Knowledge and Experience in the *Rose*

One of the primary goals of this study of the *Rose* has been to define its importance in the evolution of both medieval French and European literature. When we placed the first part of the *Rose* in the context of twelfth- and thirteen-century literature about love, we saw that although the *Rose* adapted many elements found in earlier French and Latin works, it was nonetheless the first major narrative in a vernacular language to make love the great, the only adventure experienced by the hero. Guillaume de Lorris accomplished this by setting aside the events and objects of the "real" world (the world outside the mind) and by taking us into the minds of the protagonists, which then became a new world, as real as the external one and more fascinating.

But the poet wanted to lead us not only into the minds of a young man and his beloved but also into the mental worlds of the hero's contemporaries, and even into our own. What we discovered, in this ever-expanding and ever-changing inner world disguised as a garden, were not only the feelings of the protagonists (real though these may be), but the values in which they believed. It was not ideas that interested Guillaume but ideals—the ideal Lover and the ideal Beloved whose outlines we see behind the fallible hero, the Rose, and their friends and enemies.

Through the beautiful personifications around the God of Love, through symbols such as the timeless garden, the fountain and the rose, through the God of Love's lesson, Guillaume suggests not only courtly society's ideal vision of itself but he gives us also a mysterious echo of our original unity with nature. The poet does this without ever making his hero aware of what he truly desires. Winthrop Wetherbee has summarized well the Lover's perceptions: "The Lover is in a state of constant suspension, always in danger of lapsing into a mere narcissistic infatuation with his own condition as lover, but at the same time dimly aware of a powerful symbolism that seems to invite both Lover and reader to recognize a deeper significance in his experience."[1] Later poets recognized the poetic potential of this allegorical realization of our inner world and used elements of it to express their own views of love.

Jean de Meun's continuation of the *Rose* was important for other reasons. His poem influenced European literature not because it contributed to writers' understanding of the relation of poetry to the inner world, but because it showed how poetry (narrative poetry in the vernacular, at any rate) could be a way of investigating knowledge. Jean de Meun was not concerned with what could or should be, as was his predecessor, but in how we can know what is.

At the very beginning of his poem Guillaume posited the truth of his narrative by describing it as what Macrobius called a prophetic dream. Jean did not assume the truth of his allegory; instead he wanted his narrative to ask the difficult epistemological question that intrigued and puzzled the philosophers of his time: how do we know the truth? So he opened up Guillaume's clearly outlined mental world of ideal being and brought into it fragments from all the areas of knowledge that he and his contemporaries had explored—cosmology, natural science, history, ethics. It is the way that Jean asked this difficult question about how we know something, the narrative use he made of all this knowledge, that makes his work one of the most influential in medieval literature and one of the most difficult for us to read today.

Jean saw knowledge as coming from three sources—authority, reason, and experience. The author expresses part of this epistemological theory in an "apology" that he makes at the very instant the troups of the God of Love are poised to attack the castle. After stating simply, optimistically, that "il fet bon de tout savoir" (l. 15184; it is good to know everything), Jean suggests the way to accomplish that: I haven't said anything, he claims, "qui ne soit en escrit trouvé / et par experimant prové, / ou par reson au mains provable" (ll. 15265–67; that can not be found in writing, or proved by experience, or at least provable by reason). Some years later, evidently, Jean continued to hold this tripartite conception of knowledge—books, reason, experience—for in the introduction to his translation of *The Consolation of Philosophy* he stated that Aristotle's belief that all things tend toward the good is not proved only "par l'auctorité du philosophe, mais par raison et par expériment apparant" (by the authority of the philosopher, but by reason and by clear experience). He goes on to say that a person learns to choose the proper good "par doctrine et par mainte expérience" (by doctrine and by much experience).

All three forms of knowledge are present in the *Rose,* but the reliance on authority is so pervasive that it can seem to outweigh reason and experience. The presence of authority is felt in references to respected *auctores* (authors), sometimes accompanied by direct quotations from their works, in exempla (significant stories) taken from learned Latin works or from mythology, and in unidentified paraphrases of earlier works. Whereas Guillaume only once referred to an authority (Macrobius), Jean cites Latin authors and works more that eighty times.[2] Everyone in the *Rose* quotes; even Reason feels the need to support her views with references to respected writers and to myths (see her mention of Echo: "si con tu meïsmes le prueves / par Echo, sanz querre autres prueves"; ll. 5807–8, as you yourself can prove it / by [the example of] Echo, without searching for other proofs).

Scholars of the *Rose* observed very early Jean's admiration for Latin and Greek authors and his desire to make their works relevant to his own times (an attitude that, as we have seen, was characteristic of medieval works in general). But only lately have scholars begun to see the complexity of Jean's reworking of the authorities. For example, Jean recognized authors such as Boethius and Alain de Lille as guides not only in philosophical matters but in questions of practical morality. Nature argues that clerics ought to be good people, because they can learn to be "gentis, courtais et sages" (l. 18606; refined, courtly and wise) from the books they read, which give them examples of the evils to be avoided and the good to be done. Jean himself relies on his favorite authors to substantiate what he asserts, for he has taken his very words from their books, and therefore he cannot lie—"se li preudome n'en mentirent / que les anciens livres firent" (ll. 15193–94; if the worthy men didn't lie, those who wrote the old books).

This humorous self-justification suggests, however, that the old authors could be wrong, and a closer look at what Jean does with his authors reveals ways that he undercuts their authority. Clearly he is not simply following the medieval rhetorical practice of supporting theological or philosophical arguments with citations from learned works (or worse—indulging in pedantry or padding). Jean is doing something remarkable, something, I believe, that had never been done before in a work of fiction. Although scientific and religious works in the Middle Ages routinely cite authorities and exempla, and although narrative works sometimes include mythological stories or references to authorities in their prologues or even in the course of the story (references to the legend of Narcissus, for example), no author before Jean de Meun had used learned references consistently as an element of characterization. Jean's use of citations and illustrative stories casts doubt not only on the objectivity of the speaker (as scholars have begun to recognize), it also casts doubts on our capacity to determine what the authorities really meant.

Jean undercuts in three ways the reliability of his authorities. First, the way a character in the *Rose* uses authority reveals something about the character's motivations and beliefs; it also indicates something surprising about Jean's attitude toward the authorities he cites, that they mean what we want them to mean. Scholars have recently begun to study the varied ways that Jean's characters manipulate citations and exempla for their own purposes. Thomas B. Hill, for example, has looked at the way the Old Woman misuses an example from Boethius, the caged bird longing to be free, to argue something very different from the original intent of the example, to prove, in effect, that women should be free to love whomever they choose.[3]

The second way Jean makes the reader question his authorities is to have different characters repeat the same story or citation, each time giving it a different meaning. There are two major mythological stories that are retold by more than one character, and each time the story is offered as "proof" of something that is important to the speaker. The two multipurpose exempla are Jupiter's castration of Saturn and the capture of Venus and Mars *in flagrante delicto* by an angry Vulcan. Reason first offers Jupiter's story as an example of how justice needs to be based on love (although Jean does not make it very clear why she thinks her story appropriate); the Friend talks about how the Golden Age was ended by Jupiter's aggression, as proof that we are meant to love one another without constraint; Genius cites the story for the third time as an example of the heinous crime of castration (the worst of all possible crimes, to his way of thinking).[4]

Of course, medieval authors often expounded different, even conflicting, interpretations of ancient myths and legends, but I do not know of an author before Jean de Meun who proposes different interpretations in the same work in order to reveal an essential element of a character's thinking. And he does so to lead the reader to think about the possibility that the meaning of an authority is relative to the speaker's situation.

The third way that Jean suggests the ambiguity of his authors is by allowing his readers to interpret the significance of an authority or myth. He does this by not interpreting it for them. The longest exemplum in the *Rose* is Jean's retelling of the story of Pygmalion, an expansion of Ovid's brief version to one of over 400 lines. Coming where it does at the climax of the *Rose,* this retelling of Pygmalion's story appears to be the key to the promised allegorical meaning of the *Rose.* Yet the author abstains from interpreting for us its significance. In this way he leaves the story in the reader's mind, for its many possible meanings to develop. As Regalado points out, "L'absence de glose déterminant la signification de l'*exemplum* enchâssé dans le texte augmente l'ampleur des significations possibles" (the absence of a gloss which determines the meaning of the *exemplum* set in the text increases the scope of possible meanings).[5]

As important as written authority is for Jean's theory of knowledge, reason and experience are also essential. I have already discussed the personification Reason at some length (see chapter 3). In general rationality is both a philosophy and a tool in the *Rose*; it can take the form of "other worldliness" (detachment from the things of this life), and of the methods of formal logic, as expressed by many characters in the Scholastic vocabulary of syllogism and deductive reasoning.[6] But Lady Reason finally fails to convince the Lover because she cannot overcome his respect both for authority (the God of Love) and for his own experience of love.

Experience is the form of knowledge to which scholars have given the least attention in the *Rose,* but I believe that for Jean, experience was as important as the other two sources of knowledge. In order for the Lover to discuss the value of experience, Jean interrupts the action of the *Rose* for a second time at a crucial moment (just as the Lover is about to insert his staff into the sanctuary). At this climactic moment the Lover pauses to give a short lecture in which he echoes and modifies his creator's earlier statement about it being good to know everything. But for the Lover "il fet bon de tout essaier" (l. 21521; it is good to try everything). By trying everything, a person can better enjoy (not "choose," as in the earlier passage) the good things—as the glutton does.

Since it is the Lover, not the author, who is speaking, we cannot simply take these words as the author's point of view. But the Lover argues for the value of experience in terms that reflect Scholastic thinking, thereby suggesting the general applicability of his observations.

Perhaps for these reasons the Lover's comments have often been quoted as reflecting Jean's thought. And we observed that the author himself stressed the value of experience in the preface to his translation of Boethius ("par doctrine and mainte expérience"). So Jean may have agreed with the Lover when he sums up his views in this way:

> Ainsinc va des contreres choses,
> Les unes sunt des autres gloses;
> et qui l'une an veust defenir,
> de l'autre li doit souvenir
> (ll. 21543–46)

Thus it is with contrary things, one kind glosses [explains] the other; and he who wants to define one must remember the other.

Varied experiences are therefore seen as an essential part of knowledge, since the only way to define, to really know, something is to experience its opposite.

Jean seldom lectures on the value of experience; he prefers to show its effects through his characters. And experience has made several of them wise. The Old Woman, for example, claims she has learned enough from life to hold a university chair in amorous philosophy (ll. 12771–87). Both her lecture and the Friend's are meant to convey their long experience with love—with certain kinds of love in any case. A third major character to speak from experience is False Seeming, whose long speech is aimed solely at describing the life he has led. He is the character who seems to speak the most frankly, since he is not attempting to persuade anyone of anything. He simply "tells it as it is." But we also need to remember that this character, in whom experience speaks the most openly, is the embodiment of hypocrisy, and that everything he says may be a lie. Before I discuss the unreliability of experience, however, I want to suggest two literary techniques that indicate that Jean recognizes the importance of experience.

The first, and most obvious, technique is the use of lists, of details, to convey the variety of things experienced. In the story of Pygmalion, for example, in order to express the sculptor's joy when dancing before his statue, the poet lists nineteen instruments on which Pygmalion plays. In addition, Jean repeats the name of the instrument in the form of a verb ("he flutes his flute"), so that in thirty-six lines he creates the impression of an entire orchestra, chorus, and dance group whirling in front of the beloved statue. This is one of the principal ways that Jean expands Ovid's little story, by multiplying the details that express the protagonist's experience. It is a technique used by other authors who want to encompass the richness of experience in their works, of whom the most notable example is Rabelais.

The other technique used to suggest the value of experience can be seen in the scenes from everyday life that Jean has his characters imagine. The Friend, for example, does not limit his remarks on jealousy to quoting authorities on the subject or to reasoning about its nature; he invents a jealous husband who expresses, at length and with many supporting details, his thoughts and feelings about his unhappy situation. The effect of imagining such a character is to give the reader a feeling for the husband's lived experience (however we may finally judge that experience).

Of course, the character imagined by the Friend also quotes authorities and reasons about his situation, just as his creator does. Jean has inserted one form of knowledge (authority) inside another (experience), thus suggesting a connection between them and emphasizing their relativity. For clarity, we have discussed the three forms of knowledge separately from one another, but in effect they are all related. That is, we determine the value of an exemplum or an authoritative statement by means of our experiences and our rational judgment, just as we judge the meaning of our experiences through our reason and what we have learned from other people. This is one important way that the forms of knowledge are related, through the need each has to be supplemented by the others.

Another way that the three forms of knowledge are related is through their ties to language. Not only authoritative statements but reason and experience must be verbalized in order for us to understand and communicate them. Jean returns to the problem of language a number of times, as its relation to reality appears to have been problematic for him. In the apology that we discussed earlier, he points out that "li diz doit le fet resambler" (l. 15160; the word should resemble the fact). Although Reason argues that the relation of the word to the thing is arbitrary, still she believes that she can speak properly, clearly (see ll. 7120–22). Can we ever be sure that word and thing correspond? Jean's doubts appear to reach a crisis in the speech of False Seeming— can we ever know whether his language expresses the truth?

Even more than his characters, the author himself is searching for an adequate language. Jean claims that he has taken his "words" from the Latin authors, but in reality he is searching for a way to say in French what his authorities have said in Latin, the language of wisdom and truth; he is transposing ideas into a language that has not been used to express them before. It is not surprising, then, that he feels the need to rely on his trusted authorities for help through this new territory, which Regalado has called "la totalité de l'univers créé et les extrêmes limites de l'expérience humaine" (the totality of the created universe and the extreme limits of human experience).[7] The impressive thing about Jean's use of his predecessors' ideas is not that he relied on them to express his own ideas, but that he used them so skillfully to express more than they had originally intended.

One extreme limit of human experience may be the experience of love, especially in the sexual form. It is also the experience in which the individual comes most intimately into contact with the outside world, in which experience is the most powerful and immediate. Over and over Jean links knowledge and sex, as though the two levels of experience were analogical. We have seen that both of the two important discourses on how we know occur at a moment of sexual crisis, and that in Genius's sermon the tools of writing (one of the ways of conveying knowledge) are analogies for procreation. Is Jean using the stories of Venus and Mars, and Pygmalion and his statue, in order to represent erotic scenes in a way his audience would find acceptable, thereby turning his readers into polite voyeurs?[8] Or is he doing this and more, by suggesting that "knowing" someone is, after all, symbolic of other forms of knowing?

If the sexual experience does represent for Jean the epitome of the individual's involvement with the world, we can understand why he saw the potential in Guillaume's allegory of love for expressing his own concerns about knowledge and experience—why he chose to continue the *Roman de la rose*. He took the two kinds of relationships which Guillaume had established, the Lover and the beloved, and the Lover and his mentors, and pushed them toward expressing a radical view of the individual and the primacy of individual judgment.

Jean forces the individual reader to make the final judgment in a number of ways: in his ambiguous use of citations and exempla; in omitting the final decision in the great debate between Reason, Nature, and the other authoritative voices; in pushing his characters' philosophical positions to such extremes that, in the words of Rosemund Tuve, their monologues "nail the speaker to a monstrous inadequacy."⁹ Above all, Jean asks the reader to rely on his own judgment when he gives the final word to the paradoxical character Genius, whose lecture praises literally to the skies an idea that Jean's contemporaries considered reprehensible—that all Nature asks of us is unrestrained procreation.¹⁰

The *Rose* appears finally to be saying that none of the three forms of knowledge are reliable when isolated from the others. Perhaps only faith, as a source of knowledge, can stand alone, but Jean does not discuss faith as knowledge (except briefly in Nature's speech; see ll. 19089–93). Instead, he wants to express the idea that in the end not just authority and reason but individual experience contribute to our understanding of the world. The twelfth-century romance has been described as expressing a new view of the individual, one that sees the hero forming his identity through the experiences that he undergoes.¹¹ I believe that Jean is expressing a similar idea on an intellectual level, that he is suggesting that the individual forms his or her judgment of truth through lived experiences. This may be why Jean includes in Nature's cosmology long passages on free will, on the individual's autonomy with respect to astrological forces, on true nobility residing in the individual, not in the class. Although these ideas were borrowed from Jean's authorities, they have a particularly strong appeal for him, for he found in them support for his belief in the inherent value of individual perceptions of reality.

We cannot know, of course, if Jean consciously set out to express this radical view of human knowledge, one that some of the great philosophers of his time, such as Roger Bacon, would have understood but which would not be argued widely until the Reformation over 200 years later. We do know, however, that intellectuals and writers in the thirteenth century were struggling with such questions as how we can know what is true, how philosophical truths differ from theological truths, and how the great authorities such as Aristotle can be made meaningful for a very different age. Jean has suggested his own answers to these difficult questions in his continuation of the *Rose*.

Perhaps it is this ability to speak to its readers' sense of the value of individual experience that made the *Rose* so enormously popular for so long; it helped medieval readers think about their own beliefs, about the basis of their knowledge of the world. Perhaps this also helps explain why it is a difficult work for modern readers to appreciate, for we expect to learn from a work of fiction how to perceive other people and the world, how to understand and admire, but not how to know. But today the growing interest in cognitive theory, in how we know what we know, suggests that the question of knowledge fascinates us more than ever. Perhaps the *Rose* can still help us to think about how we know each other and the world.

Notes and References

Chapter One

1. The Old French edition used for this study is by Felix Lecoy, *Le Roman de la rose,* 3 vols. (Paris: Honoré Champion, 1965–75); hereafter cited in the text by page or line references. The translations are mine.

2. The most recent modern translation, by Charles Dahlberg (*The Romance of the Rose by Guillaume de Lorris and Jean de Meun,* [Princeton: Princeton University Press, 1971]), is based on the Langlois edition (see note 3 below), but the translator gives a table of concordances that allows the reader to find lines from the Lecoy edition in the translation.

3. Ernest Langlois, *Le Roman de la Rose, par Guillaume de Lorris et Jean de Meun, publié d'après les manuscrits,* 5 vols. (1914–24; reprint, Geneva: Johnson Reprints, 1965), 1:2, 17–20; hereafter cited in the text as *L.*

4. See discussion of authenticity by Langlois, *Roman,* 1:20–21, and by Aimée Celeste Bourneuf, "The 'Testament' of Jean de Meung; Vatican MS. 367" (Ph. D. diss., Fordham University, 1956).

5. The original name of an allegorical character is given after the translation if there is no simple English equivalent, such as for *papelardie. Papelardie* probably comes from Old French *paper,* "to eat," plus *lard,* and suggests a religious hypocrite who eats meat on meatless days. It was a word coined in the thirteenth century to refer specifically to hypocritical clerics; later it came to mean hypocrisy of any kind. (See "papelardie," in Robert's *Dictionnaire alphabétique et analogique du français* [Paris: Dictionnaires Le Robert, 1962]).

6. *Deduit* in Old French refers to physical pleasure or amusement, especially amorous play (see ll. 2472–73: "que mieuz vaut de li un regarz / que d'autre li deduit entiers;" that one look from her is worth more / than the complete enjoyment of another woman). Dahlberg translates Deduit as Diversion; the other modern translator, Harry W. Robbins, calls him Sir Mirth; see *The Romance of the Rose by Guillaume de Lorris and Jean de Meun* (New York: Dutton, 1962).

7. *Dangiers* in Old French can refer to a husband's power over his wife (or to anyone who is an obstacle to love) or to resistance in general. In the *Rose* it appears to refer to the young woman's reluctance in love. See the discussion by C. S. Lewis, *The Allegory of Love* (Oxford: Oxford University Press, 1936), 123–24, 364–66 and Douglas Kelly, *Medieval Imagination: Rhetoric and the Poetry of Courtly Love* (Madison: University of Wisconsin Press, 1978), 85–91.

8. Although Warm Welcome represents an aspect of the young woman's feelings, and although the advice the Old Woman gives is meant for a

woman, the allegorical character is a male because the noun *accueil* is masculine.

9. Ernest Langlois, *Les manuscrits du "Roman de la rose:" Description et classement* (1910; reprint, Geneva: Slatkine Reprints, 1974). See also Marc-René Jung, "Ein Fragment des *Rosenromans* in der Stiftsbibliothek Engelberg," *Vox Romanica* 24 (1965): 234–37.

10. Thomas E. Kelly and Thomas H. Ohlgren, "Paths to Memory: Iconographic Indices to *Roman de la Rose* and *Prose Lancelot* Manuscripts in the Bodleian Library," *Visual Resources* 3, no. 1 (1983):1–15. An early study of the manuscripts can be found in Alfred Kuhn's "Die Illustration des *Rosenromans,*" *Jahrbuch der Kunsthistorischen Sammlungen der allerhöchsten Kaiserhauses* 31 (1913–14): 1–66.

11. John V. Fleming, *The "Roman de la Rose": A Study in Allegory and Iconography* (Princeton: Princeton University Press, 1969); Rosemond Tuve, *Allegorical Imagery: Some Mediaeval Books and their Posterity* (Princeton: Princeton University Press, 1966).

12. Unfortunately no facsimile of a *Rose* manuscript has been published. Fleming's book on the *Rose* and Dahlberg's translation reproduce a number of miniatures. For more information on the manuscripts and miniatures, see Maxwell Luria, *A Reader's Guide to the "Roman de la Rose"* (Hamden, Conn.: Archon Books, 1982), 14–16.

13. F. W. Bourdillon, *The Early Editions of the Roman de la Rose* (London: Bibliographical Society, 1906). Luria summarizes the history of the early editions in *Reader's Guide,* 17–21.

Chapter Two

1. See the important article by Robert Guiette, "D'une poésie formelle en France au moyen âge" (1949; reprinted in *Questions de littérature,* Romanica Gandensia 8 [Ghent, 1960], 9–23); Kelly, *Medieval Imagination,* xi–xvi; and Italo Siciliano, *François Villon et les thèmes poétiques du moyen âge* (Paris: A. Colin, 1934).

2. Gaston Paris, "Etudes sur les romans de la Table Ronde: Lancelot du Lac," *Romania* 10 (1881): 465–96; 12 (1883): 459–34; 16 (1887): 100–101. A collection of articles on "courtly love" is given in *The Meaning of Courtly Love,* ed. F. X. Newman (Albany: State University of New York Press, 1968). See also William Calin, "Defense and Illustration of *Fin' Amor*: Some Polemical Comments on the Robertsonian Approach," in *The Expansion and Transformation of Courtly Literature,* ed. Nathanial B. Smith and Joseph T. Snow (New York: Pantheon Books, 1953), 33–49.

3. Lewis, *Allegory,* 4.

4. *The Poetry of William VII, Count of Poitiers, IX Duke of Aquitaine,* ed. and trans. Gerald A. Bond (New York: Garland, 1982).

5. A good selection of songs is given in *Lyrics of the Troubadours and*

Trouvères, trans. Frederick Goldin (Garden City, N. Y.: Anchor Press, 1973); the introduction is also informative.

6. Ibid., 103, 127.

7. Ibid., 127.

8. Ibid., 39.

9. Ibid., 127.

10. In addition to Lewis's *Allegory of Love,* see Jean Batany, *Approches du "Roman de la Rose"* (Paris: Bordas, 1974), 15.

11. Charles Muscatine, "The Emergence of Psychological Allegory in Old French Romance," *PMLA* 68 (1953): 1160–82; see also Marc-René Jung, *Etudes sur le poème allégorique en France au moyen âge* (Berne: Eds. Francke, 1971), 170–91.

12. Muscatine, "Emergence," 1179–80.

13. Andreas Capellanus, *The Art of Courtly Love,* trans. John Jay Parry (1941; reprint, New York: Frederick Ungar, 1959).

14. Ibid., 80.

15. See ibid., 81–82, 184–86.

16. Ibid., 88.

17. Langlois, *Origines et sources du Roman de la Rose* (1890; reprint, Geneva: Slatkine Reprints, 1973), 6–15, 21–23, 26–31. Langlois discusses a number of other allegorical love poems which he claims were sources for the *Roman de la rose,* but most of these are now believed to postdate the *Rose.* Therefore Langlois's work must be read with care. A new study of the sources of Guillaume's love allegory would be very useful.

18. See Lewis, *Allegory,* 6–8.

19. See Peter Dronke, *Medieval Latin and the rise of European love-lyric,* 2 vols. (Oxford: Clarendon Press, 1965–66), 1:192–220; Winthrop Wetherbee, *Platonism and Poetry in the Twelfth Century: The Literary Influence of the School of Chartres* (Princeton: Princeton University Press, 1972), 11–14.

20. For Envy and Narcissus, see *Metamorphoses,* 2. 775–82, 3. 344–502; for the two arrows, 1. 468–71. A number of articles have been written on Guillaume's fountain and version of the Narcissus myth; see, for example, Erich Köhler, "Narcisse, la Fontaine d'Amour et Guillaume de Lorris," in *L'humanisme médiéval dans les littératures romanes du XIIᵉ au XIVᵉ siècles,* ed. A. Fourrier (Paris: Klincksieck, 1964), 147–66.

21. Luria, *Reader's Guide,* 37–38.

22. Jung, *Etudes,* 31.

23. Ibid., 31–33. For a perceptive analysis of allegory in the *Psychomachia,* see Carolynn Van Dyke's *The Fiction of Truth: Structures of Meaning in Narrative and Dramatic Allegory* (Ithaca, N. Y.: Cornell University Press, 1985), pt. 1.

24. Lewis, *Allegory,* 78–90.

25. Wetherbee, *Platonism,* 83–84; see also W. H. Stahl, "To a Better Understanding of Martianus Capella," *Speculum* 40 (1965):102–15.

26. For a more detailed summary, see Wetherbee, *Platonism,* 83–90, and Jung, *Etudes,* 35ff.

27. Ibid., 90.

28. Boethius, *The Consolation of Philosophy* trans. V. E. Watts (Harmondsworth, Middlesex, England: Penguin Books, 1969), 8.

29. A helpful discussion of the problem of studying an earlier author's influence on Jean de Meun is given by Daniel Poirion, "Alain de Lille et Jean de Meun," in *Alain de Lille, Gautier de Châtillon, Jakemart Giélée et leur temps,* comp. H. Roussel and F. Suard (Lille: Presses Universitaires de Lille, 1980), 135–51.

30. Alain de Lille, *The Plaint of Nature,* trans. and commentary by James J. Sheridan (Toronto: Pontifical Institute of Medieval Studies, 1980), 31–35.

31. Ibid., 130.

32. Ibid., 220.

33. Langlois, *Origines,* 95.

34. Winthrop Wetherbee, "The Literal and the Allegorical: Jean de Meun and the 'de Planctu Naturae,'" *Mediaeval Studies* 33 (1971):264–91. See also Wetherbee, *Platonism,* 255–66, and Lucie Polak, "Plato, Nature and Jean de Meun," *Reading Mediaeval Studies* 3 (1977):80–103.

35. Wetherbee, "Literal" 272.

36. Ibid., 281.

37. For more analysis of the works of Alain and Bernard, see Wetherbee, *Platonism,* 152–219, Batany, *Approches,* 34–37, and Marc-René Jung, *Etudes,* especially 72–89, on the interpretation of the *Anticlaudianus* and its possible influence on Guillaume de Lorris.

38. See Ernst Robert Curtius, *European Literature and the Latin Middle Ages,* trans. Willard R. Trask (New York: Pantheon Books, 1953); Helmut Hatzfeld, "La mystique naturiste de Jean de Meung," *Wissenschaftliche Zeitschrift der Friedrich-Schiller-Universität Iena* 5 (1955–56):259–69.

39. Hans Robert Jauss, "La transformation de la forme allégorique entre 1130 et 1240: d'Alain de Lille à Guillaume de Lorris," in *L'humanisme médiéval,* 107–46. See also Jauss's contribution to *La littérature didactique, allégorique et satirique,* in *Grundriss der romanischen Literaturen des Mittelalters* (Heidelberg: Winter, 1968), vol. 6, pt. 2, 265–80.

40. Jauss, "La transformation," 121.

41. See ibid., 143–44.

42. Macrobius, *Commentary on the Dream of Scipio,* trans. William Harris Stahl (New York: Columbia University Press, 1952), 39–40.

43. Constance B. Hieatt, *The Realism of Dream Visions: The Poetic Exploitation of the Dream Experience in Chaucer and his Contemporaries* (The Hague: Mouton, 1967), 21.

44. Ibid., 20.

45. For a discussion of the literary elements of the dream in the *Rose*, see Terence Wright, "Le Cadre du rêve dans le *Roman de la Rose*," *Chimères* 15 (Summer 1981): 43–53; Anthony Colin Spearing, *Medieval Dream-Poetry* (Cambridge: Cambridge University Press, 1976).

46. Jauss, "La transformation," 145–46.

47. Fernand van Steenberghen, *La Philosophie au XIII*ᵉ *siècle* (Louvain: Publications Universitaires, 1966). A useful survey of the influence of Aristotelian philosophy on the thirteenth century can be found in Frederick Copleston, *A History of Philosophy,* vol. 2, *Mediaeval Philosophy* (Garden City, N. Y.: Image Books, 1962), part 2, Albert the Great to Duns Scotus.

48. Langlois, *Origines,* 109; Gérard M. Paré, *Les idées et les lettres au XIII*ᵉ *siècle: Le Roman de la Rose* (Montreal: University of Montreal, 1947), 13. See also Mary Katherine Tillman, "Scholastic and Averroistic Influences on the *Roman de la Rose*," *Annuale medievale* 11 (1970):89–106.

49. Tillman, "Scholastic," 105.

50. Paré, *Les idées,* 340; Alan M. F. Gunn, *The Mirror of Love: A Reinterpretation of the Romance of the Rose* (Lubbock: Texas Tech Press, 1952), especially bk. 2, "The Rhetoric of the Rose."

Chapter Three

1. While it would be impossible to cite all the important works on allegory, the following are essential: Angus Fletcher, *Allegory: The Theory of a Symbolic Mode* (Ithaca, N. Y.: Cornell University Press, 1964); Maureen Quilligan, *The Language of Allegory: Defining the Genre* (Ithaca, N. Y.: Cornell University Press, 1979); Tuve, *Allegorical Imagery*; and Van Dyke, *Fiction of Truth,* to which this discussion of allegory is much indebted.

2. Van Dyke, *Fiction of Truth,* 17.

3. Quoted in ibid., 19.

4. See Fletcher, *Allegory,* 75.

5. Morton W. Bloomfield, "Allegory as Interpretation," *New Literary History* 3 (1972):301.

6. Van Dyke, *Fiction of Truth,* 39.

7. Lewis, *Allegory,* 48.

8. A striking example of this unfortunate normative approach is Michel Defourny's article, "Observations sur la première partie du *Roman de la Rose*," in which he faults Guillaume de Lorris for not following the supposed "lois du genre allégorique" (laws of the genre of allegory) (in *Mélanges offerts à Rita Lejeune, professeur à l'Université de Liège* [Gembloux: Duculot, 1969], 2:1169). Defourny finds three "incoherences" in the first part, one of which is the surprising presence of Jealousy and her troops in this earthly paradise. The reader, however, has no problem with this sudden enlarging of the garden (this is, after all, a dream as well as an allegory). Jean Batany also reproaches

Guillaume for mixing in real characters with his abstractions (in "Paradigmes lexicaux et structures littéraires au Moyen Age," *Revue d'histoire littéraire de la France* 70 [1970]:827–28).

9. Tuve, *Allegorical Imagery*, 239.

10. See Lewis, *Allegory*, 129; Fleming, *Roman de la Rose*, 133; Van Dyke, *Fiction of Truth*, 77–78; René Louis, *Le Roman de la Rose: Essai d'interprétation de l'allégorisme érotique* (Paris: Honoré Champion, 1974), 12.

11. Jean-Charles Payen, "A Semiological Study of Guillaume de Lorris," *Yale French Studies* 51 (1974):170–84.

12. Van Dyke, *Fiction of Truth*, 63.

13. W. T. H. Jackson, "Allegory and Allegorization," in *The Challenge of the Medieval Text* (New York: Columbia University Press, 1985), 160; Robert Worth Frank, Jr., "The Art of Reading Medieval Personification-Allegory," *ELH, A Journal of English Literary History* 20 (1953): 237–50. Paul Zumthor distinguishes three functions of allegory, the didactic, the deictic, and the narrative, in "Narrative and Anti-Narrative: *Le Roman de la Rose,*" *Yale French Studies* 51 (1974):185–204; see especially 191–94.

14. Jackson, "Allegory," 161.

15. Other generic frames can serve allegory, such as the beast fable in Orwell's *Animal Farm*.

16. Jackson, "Allegory," 166.

17. See the discussion by Rita Lejeune, "A propos de la structure du *Roman de la Rose* de Guillaume de Lorris," in *Etudes de langue et littérature du moyen âge offertes à Félix Lecoy* (Paris: Honoré Champion, 1973), 347–48, and reply by Gertrud Meyer, "A propos de la structure du *Roman de la Rose* de Guillaume de Lorris," in *Romanistische Zeitschrift für Literaturgeschichte* 2 (1978):265–68. For an approach to the question based on a grammatical analysis of the end of part one, see Paul Strohm's "Guilllaume as Narrator and Lover in the *Roman de la Rose,*" *Romanic Review* 59 (1968):3–9.

18. Paul Piehler, *The Visionary Landscape: A Study in Medieval Allegory* (Montreal: McGill-Queen's University Press, 1971); see especially 98–110. Piehler's discussion of the first part of the *Rose* deals only with the topos of the garden, not with Guillaume's figures of authority. Jane Chance Nitzsche relates the authoritative guide to the role of Genius as messenger of higher truth; see *The Genius Figure in Antiquity and the Middle Ages* (New York: Columbia University Press, 1975), 62–63. For a discussion of the initiation pattern, see Daniel Poirion, *Le Roman de la Rose* (Paris: Hatier, 1973), 69–73; Jacques Ribard, "Introduction à une étude polysémique du *Roman de la Rose* de Guillaume de Lorris," in *Etudes de langue*, 519–28.

19. Piehler, *Visionary Landscape*, 4.

20. Ibid., 103.

21. Gunn, *Mirror of Love*, pt. 5.

22. Tuve, *Allegorical Imagery*, 49.

23. Ibid., 241, 245.

24. Marc-René Jung, "Jean de Meun et l'Allégorie," *Cahiers de l'Association Internationale des Etudes Françaises* 28 (1976):30.

25. On satire of the religious orders in medieval literature, see Penn R. Szittya, *The Antifraternal Tradition in Medieval Literature* (Princeton: Princeton University Press, 1986), especially 184–90. On False Seeming specifically, see the notes to Lecoy's edition, 2:280–82; Batany, *Approches,* 97–112.

26. Tillman, "Scholastic," 96.

27. Lewis, *Allegory,* 115.

28. Ibid., 113, 115.

29. Ibid., 135.

30. Tuve, *Allegorical Imagery,* 248 n. 10.

31. Poirion, *Le Roman de la Rose,* 83.

32. Fleming, *Roman de la Rose,* 59.

33. Quilligan, "Allegory," 163.

34. Kelly, *Medieval Imagination,* 24.

35. Frank, "Allegory," 342.

36. Kelly, *Medieval Imagination,* 58.

37. For an analysis of the personifications in terms of the *actants* of A. J. Greimas's semantic theory, see Batany, *Approches,* 42–43.

38. Kelly, *Medieval Imagination,* 74–75.

39. Ibid., 77.

40. See Fleming, *Roman de la Rose,* 32.

41. The garden as a topos in classical and medieval literature has been discussed by many scholars. See, for example, Curtius, *European Literature,* 183–200; Fleming, *Romance de la Rose,* chap. 2.

42. Lewis, *Allegory,* 119.

43. Larry H. Hillman, "Another Look into the Mirror Perilous; the Role of the Crystals in the *Roman de la Rose,*" *Romania* 101 (1980):238. See also Sylvia Huot, "From *Roman de la Rose* to *Roman de la Poire*: The Ovidian Tradition and the Poetics of Courtly Literature," *Mediaevalia et Humanistica,* n.s. 13 (1985):95–111.

44. See Daniel Poirion, "Genèse et finalité de la pensée allégorique au Moyen Age," *Revue de métaphysique et de morale* 19 (1973):466–79.

45. Van Dyke, *Fiction of Truth,* 78, 84.

46. Lewis, *Allegory,* 141.

47. Tuve, *Allegorical Imagery,* 246.

48. Jauss and Frappier, "Transformation," 145–46.

49. Alan Gunn, in *The Mirror of Love,* was the first to argue that these speeches are not digressions, and he supported this position with detailed analysis of medieval rhetorical practice.

50. Vladimir Rossman, *Perspectives of Irony in Medieval French Literature* (The Hague: Mouton, 1975), 157.

51. Fleming, *Reason and the Lover* (Princeton, N. J.: Princeton University Press, 1984); Tuve, *Allegorical Imagery,* 261; Van Dyke, *Fiction of Truth,* 85–87.

52. Charles Muscatine, "Courtly Literature and Vulgar Language," in *Court and Poet: Selected Proceedings of the Third Congress of the International Courtly Literature Society,* ed. Glyn S. Burgess (Liverpool: Francis Cairns, 1981), 1–19.

53. Maureen Quilligan, "Words and Sex: The Language of Allegory in the *De Planctu Naturae,* the *Roman de la Rose,* and Book III of the *Faerie Queene,*" *Allegorica* 1, no. 1 (1977):199. See also Wetherbee, "Literal," 272–73; Thomas D. Hill, "Narcissus, Pygmalion, and the Castration of Saturn: Two Mythographical Themes in the *Roman de la Rose,*" *Studies in Philology* 71 (1974):404-26.

54. Quilligan, "Words," 199.

55. As does Pierre-Yves Badel, "Raison, 'fille de Dieu,' et le Rationalisme de Jean de Meun," in *Mélanges de langue et de littérature du Moyen Age et de la Renaissance offerts à Jean Frappier,* 2 vols. (Geneva: Droz, 1970), 1:40–52.

56. Hill, "Narcissus," 416.

57. Ibid., 426.

58. A. O. Lovejoy and G. Boas, *Primitivism and Related Ideas in Antiquity* (Baltimore: Johns Hopkins Press, 1935), 447–56. See also R. G. Collingwood, *The Idea of Nature* (New York: Oxford University Press, 1960).

59. Aristotle, *Metaphysics,* 1015a.15, in *The Complete Works of Aristotle,* trans. W. D. Ross, vol. 8 (Oxford: Oxford University Press, 1928). For a discussion of the philosophical background of Natura, see the first chapter of George Economou, *The Goddess Natura in Medieval Literature* (Cambridge, Mass.: Harvard University Press, 1972).

60. J. A. W. Bennett, *The Parlement of Foules* (Oxford: Clarendon Press, 1957), 194–95.

61. C. S. Lewis, *The Discarded Image* (Cambridge: Cambridge University Press, 1964), 39.

62. Economou, *Goddess,* 58.

63. See Aldo D. Scaglione, *Nature and Love in the Late Middle Ages* (Berkeley: University of California Press, 1963).

64. An excellent history of the Church's attitudes toward sexuality and procreation is given by John T. Noonan, Jr., in *Contraception: A History of Its Treatment by the Catholic Theologians and Canonists* (Cambridge, Mass.: Harvard University Press, 1966).

65. See note 18 above. My summary of the concept's history is based on Nitzsche's work. For further discussion, see E. C. Knowlton, "The Allegorical Figure Genius," *Classical Philology* 15 (1920):380–84 and "Genius as an Allegorical Figure," *Modern Language Notes* 39 (1924):89–95; Pierre-Yves Badel,

Le "Roman de la Rose" au XIVe siècle: Étude de la réception de l'oeuvre (Geneva: Droz, 1980), 29–51.

66. See the note to lines 19569–98 in the Lecoy edition; also Noonan, *Contraception,* 276ff.; F. Van Steenberghen, *La Philosophie,* chap. 9.

67. In a note to lines 19569–98, Lecoy refers to "la sympathie de notre auteur pour certains mouvements d'opinion et de pensée qui tombaient sous le coup de la condamnation prononcée le 7 mars 1277" (the sympathy felt by our author for certain movements of thought and opinion which were the target of the condemnation issued 7 March 1277); see also M. M. Gorce, *Le Roman de la Rose: Texte essentiel de la scolastique courtoise* (Paris: Eds. Montaigne, 1933).

68. Fleming, for example, sees Genius as "man's *nautralis concupiscentia*" (*Roman de la Rose,* 214), but he nonetheless accepts the authority of the second part of the sermon, especially as a condemnation of courtly love.

69. Denise N. Baker, "The Priesthood of Genius: A Study of the Medieval Tradition," *Speculum* 51 (1976):277–91.

70. Gunn, *Mirror of Love,* 385, n., 404–5, n.

Chapter Four

1. Lewis, *Allegory,* 157.

2. Fleming, *Roman de la Rose,* vi.

3. Lewis, *Allegory,* 157.

4. The principle works on late medieval allegorical poetry in France are Badel, *Le Roman de la Rose*; Jauss, *La littérature didactique,* in particular pt. 1, 146–244, and pt. 2, 265–80; Daniel Poirion, *Le prince et le poète: l'évolution du lyrisme courtois de Guillaume de Machaut à Charles D'Orléans* (Paris: Presses Universitaires de France, 1965). See also Luria, *Reader's Guide,* 59–74.

5. Badel, *Roman de la Rose,* 331.

6. Spearing, *Medieval Dream Poetry,* 41–47.

7. R. W. V. Elliott, "Chaucer's Reading," in *Chaucer's Mind and Art,* ed. A. C. Cawley (Edinburgh: Oliver & Boyd, 1969), 65.

8. Nicole de Margival, *Le dit de la Panthère d'Amours,* ed. Henry A. Todd (Paris: Firmin Didot, 1983); Messire Thibaut, *Li romanz de la poire,* ed. Friedrich Stehlich (Halle: Max Niemeyer, 1881). See Huot's perceptive comparison of the *Rose* and the *Poire* in "From *Roman de la Rose* to *Roman de la Poire.*"

9. See Badel, *Roman de la Rose,* 332–53, for a more detailed discussion of the variables found in dream poems.

10. *Le dit du vergier,* in *Les oeuvres de Guillaume de Machaut,* ed. Ernest Hoepffner, 3 vols. (Paris: Firmin-Didot, 1908–21), 1:13–56.

11. Machaut's life and works are discussed by James Wimsatt in *Chaucer and the French Love Poets: The Literary Background of the "Book of the Duchess"*

(Chapel Hill: University of North Carolina Press, 1968). William Calin compares Machaut's poetry to the *Roman de la rose* in "Problèmes de technique narrative au Moyen-Age: *Le Roman de la Rose* et Guillaume de Machaut," in *Mélanges de langue et littérature françaises du Moyen-Age offerts à Pierre Jonin,* Senefiance no. 7 (Aix-en-Provence: CUERMA, 1979), 127–38.

12. Jean de Condé, *La messe des oiseaux,* ed. Jacques Ribard (Geneva: Droz, 1970); the *Echecs d'amour,* analysis and excerpts in Ernst Sieper, *Les Echecs amoureaux: Eine altfranzösische Nachahmung des Rosenromans* (Weimar: E. Felber, 1889).

13. Muscatine, "Emergence," 1161.

14. Wimsatt, *Chaucer,* 30–31.

15. Badel, *Roman de la Rose,* 226–59.

16. Ibid., 165.

17. Ibid., 373.

18. Thomas D. Hill, "La Vieille's Digression on Free Love: A Note on Rhetorical Structure in the *Roman de la rose,*" *Romance Notes* 8 (1966-67):113–15.

19. Quoted by Badel, *Roman de la Rose,* 78.

20. *Le Débat sur "le Roman de la Rose,"* ed. Eric Hicks (Paris: Honoré Champion, 1977). A good translation of the documents and an introduction to the debate can be found in *La Querelle de la Rose: Letters and Documents,* ed. Joseph L. Baird and John R. Kane (Chapel Hill: North Carolina Studies in the Romance Languages and Literatures, 1978). See also the detailed discussion by Badel, *Roman de la Rose,* 411–89.

21. Enid McLeod, *The Order of the Rose: The Life and Ideas of Christine de Pizan* (Totowa, N. J.: Rowan & Littlefield, 1976). See Baird and Kane, eds., *La Querelle,* 15–19, for a fair evaluation of Christine's role in the debate.

22. See Badel, *Roman de la Rose,* 422–23.

23. On the question of "decorum," see Lionel Friedman, "'Jean de Meung,' Antifeminism, and 'Bourgeois Realism,'" *Modern Philology* 57 (1959):13–23.

24. André Lanly, "Villon, le *Roman de la Rose* et le *Testament* de Jean de Meun," in *Hommage à Jean Seguy,* 2 vols. (Toulouse: Université de Toulouse—Le Mirail, 1978), 1:238. Louis Thuasne, *Villon et Rabelais* (Paris: Librairie Fischbacher, 1911); Italo Siciliano, *Les mésaventures posthumes de maître Françoys Villon* (Paris: Picard, 1973). See also Siciliano, *François Villon,* and David Kuhn, *La poétique de François Villon* (Paris: A. Colin, 1967).

25. Jean Rychner and Albert Henry, eds., *Le Testament Villon,* vol. 1 (Geneva: Droz, 1974), l. 1178.

26. Ibid., ll. 113–14.

27. See Johan Huizinga, *The Waning of the Middle Ages* (Garden City, N. Y.: Doubleday Anchor Books, 1954), chap. 9.

28. See, for example, Tuve, *Allegorical Imagery,* 243.

29. Jean-Charles Payen, "Diderot et le Moyen Age: Recherches complé-

mentaires," *Licorne* 6, no. 2 (1982):239–52; "Jean-Jacques Rousseau et le *Roman de la Rose*," *Revue philosophique de la France et de l'étranger* 168 (1978):351–56.

30. On Gower, see for example George Economou, "The Character Genius in Alain de Lille, Jean de Meun, and John Gower," *Chaucer Review* 4 (1970):203–10; see also Donald Schueller, "Gower's Characterization of Genius in the *Confessio Amantis*," *Chaucer Review* 4 (1972):240–56. Quilligan examines the relation of Spenser's *The Faerie Queene* to the works of Alain de Lille and Jean de Meun in "Words and Sex." See also Tuve, *Allegorical Imagery*, 279–82.

31. The major studies of Chaucer and the *Romance of the rose* are the following: Dean Spruill Fansler, *Chaucer and the Roman de la Rose* (1914; reprint, Gloucester, Mass.: Peter Smith, 1965); Charles Muscatine, *Chaucer and the French Tradition* (Berkeley: University of California Press, 1957); and Wimsatt, *Chaucer*. In *Chaucer, Sources and Backgrounds* (New York: Oxford University Press, 1977), Robert P. Miller gives relevant excerpts from the *Rose*.

32. Luria, *Reader's Guide*, 75.

33. See Wimsatt, *Chaucer*, chap. 1; R. A. Shoaf, "'Mutatio Amoris': 'Penitentia' and the Form of the *Book of the Duchess*," *Genre* 14, no. 2 (1981):163–89.

34. An excellent introduction to the *Romaunt* can be found in Ronald Sutherland, *The Romaunt of the Rose and Le Roman de la Rose: A Parallel-Text Edition* (Berkeley: University of California Press, 1968).

35. Etienne Gustave Sandras, *Etude sur Chaucer considéré comme imitateur des trouvères* (Paris: A. Durand. 1859).

36. Walter W. Skeat, ed., *Complete Works of Geoffrey Chaucer*, 2d ed., 7 vols. (Oxford: Clarendon Press, 1899); Emil Koeppel, "Chauceriana," *Anglia* 14 (1892):227–67. The notes to F. N. Robinson, Jr.'s edition contain much information about Chaucer's sources: *The Works of Geoffrey Chaucer*, 2d ed. (Boston: Houghton Mifflin, 1957).

37. Lisi Cipriani, "Studies in the Influence of the *Romance of the Rose* upon Chaucer," *PMLA* 22 (1907):552–95; Fansler, *Chaucer*. A more useful approach to the question of literary influence can be found in Wimsatt, *Chaucer*.

38. Lynn King Morris, *Chaucer Source and Analogue Criticism* (New York: Garland Publishing Co., 1985), especially 540–42.

39. James Wimsatt, "Chaucer and French Poetry," in *Geoffrey Chaucer*, ed. D. S. Brewer (Athens: Ohio University Press, 1975), 109–36. This is one of the best short introductions to the question of the influence of the *Rose* on Chaucer.

40. Ibid., 114–16.

41. Cipriani, "Studies," 583.

42. "Pardoner's Prologue," in *Works of Geoffrey Chaucer*, ed. Robinson, ll. 400–403.

43. Ibid., ll. 415–16.

44. Wimsatt, "Chaucer," 131.

45. Earl Jeffrey Richards, Dante and the "Roman de la Rose": An Investigation into the Vernacular Narrative Context of the "Commedia" (Tubingen: Max Niemeyer, 1981), 22. See also Luigi Foscolo Benedetto, Il "Roman de la Rose" e la letteratura italiana (Halle: M. Niemeyer, 1910).

46. Richards, Dante, 29.

47. On the debate over Fiore, see Gianfranco Contini, "Un nodo della cultura medievale: La serie Roman de la Rose-Fiore-Divina Commedia," Lettere italiane 25 (1973):162–89; Luigi Vanossi, Dante e il "Roman de la Rose": Saggio sul "Fiore" (Florence: L. S. Olschki, 1979).

48. See the discussion by Richards, Dante, 35–36.

49. Ibid., 33.

50. Ibid., 74–77.

51. John Took, "Dante and the Roman de la Rose," Italian Studies 37 (1982):1–25.

52. Richards, Dante, 85.

53. Joseph R. Strayer, ed., Dictionary of the Middle Ages (New York: Charles Scribner's Sons, 1982), 101.

54. Richards, Dante, 67.

Chapter Five

1. See Charles Dahlberg's more sophisticated efforts to make the figure of Dangier (Resistance) at the foot of the Lover's bed in some opening miniatures a reference to Joseph at Mary's bedside, in "Love and the Roman de la Rose," Speculum 44 (1969):568–84. See also Luria, Reader's Guide, 203–4.

2. See Tuve, Allegorical Imagery, 237–84.

3. Silvio Baridon, ed., Le Roman de la Rose par Guillaume de Lorris et Jean de Meung dans la version attribuée à Clément Marot (Milan: Istituto Editoriale Cisalpino, 1954–57), 1:89.

4. Pierre Ronsard, preface to the Franciade; sonnet 136 of Amours de 1552 (in Gustave Cohen, Le Roman de la Rose [Paris: Centre de Documentation Universitaire, 1973], 3–4). See also Joachim du Bellay's Défense et illustration de la langue française, bk. 2, chap. 2.

5. See Nathan Edelman's Attitudes of Seventeenth-Century France toward the Middle Ages (New York: King's Crown Press, 1946); Lionel Gossman, Medievalism and the Ideologies of the Enlightenment: The World and Work of Lacurne de Sainte-Palaye (Baltimore: Johns Hopkins Press, 1968).

6. Marc-René Jung gives a long, detailed summary of Rose scholarship in "Der Rosenroman in der Kritik seit dem 18. Jahrhundert," Romanische Forschungen 78 (1966):203–52; see 203–13 on the eighteenth century.

7. Michel Defourny, "Le Roman de la Rose à travers l'histoire et la philosophie," Marche romane 17 (1967):56; see also Jung, "Der Rosenroman," 213.

8. M. Méon, ed., *Le Roman de la Rose par Guillame de Lorris et Jehan de Meung: Nouvelle edition, revue et corrigée sur les meilleurs et plus anciens manuscrits,* 4 vols. (Paris: P. Didot l'aîné, 1814).

9. Gaston Paris, *La littérature française au Moyen Age,* 2d ed. (Paris: Hachette, 1890).

10. Paulin Paris, *Histoire littéraire de la France,* 23 (1856):1-61.

11. Gaston Paris, *La littérature,* 166.

12. See, for example, Langlois, *Origines,* 95–97.

13. Ibid., 94.

14. Gustave Lanson, "Un naturaliste du XIIIe siècle: Jean de Meung," *Revue bleue politique et littéraire* 2 (1894):35–41.

15. Ibid., 36.

16. Ibid., 35, 37.

17. Bibliographical information will be given in this chapter only for those works not referred to elsewhere; information on most of the scholars discussed here can be found in the notes to earlier chapters or in the selected bibliography. In addition to the studies of *Rose* criticism by Defourny and Jung mentioned above, surveys of criticism can be found in Badel, *Le Roman de la Rose,* 1–13, and in Susan Ramsey, "Etat présent du *Roman de la Rose,*" *Chimères* 9 (Summer 1975):14–28. Many books on the *Rose,* such as those by Gunn (*Mirror of Love*) and Fleming (*Reason and the Lover*), begin with discussions of earlier criticism.

18. Poirion, *Roman de la Rose,* 80–86.

19. See the discussion by Dahlberg, *Romance,* 5–10.

20. Lewis, *Allegory,* 137.

21. An exception to this tendency is the excellent collection of essays on Guillaume de Lorris's *Rose* published recently, *Etudes sur le Roman de la Rose de Guillaume de Lorris,* ed. Jean Dufournet (Geneva: Editions Slatkine, 1984).

22. Lewis, *Allegory,* 154.

23. Gunn, *Mirror of Love,* 317.

24. See the review of Gunn's book by C. S. Lewis, in *Medium Aevum* 22 (1953):27–31.

25. Robertson, *Preface,* 104.

26. Jean-Charles Payen, "L'espace et le temps dans le *Roman de la Rose,*" in *Etudes de langue et de littérature française offertes à André Lanly* (Nancy: University of Nancy II, 1980), 292–93.

27. Gustave Cohen, *Le Roman de la Rose* (1928; reprint, Paris: Centre de Documentation Universitaire, 1973), 208.

28. Marcel Françon, "Jean de Meun et les origines du naturalisme de la Renaissance," *PMLA* 59 (1944):624–45; see especially 628. F. W. Müller, *Der Rosenroman und der lateinische Averroïsmus des 13. Jahrhunderts* (Frankfurt-am-Main: Vittorio Klostermann, 1947).

29. Françon, "Jean de Meun," 628.

30. Gunn, *Mirror of Love,* chap. 11. This approach is based on Arthur O. Lovejoy's *Great Chain of Being* (Cambridge, Mass.: Harvard University

Press, 1936). Unfortunately, Gunn's argument is weakened by a misinterpretation of Nature's remark about "la bele chaene doree" (l. 16756; the beautiful golden chain), which refers to the stability of the universe under Nature, not to its plenitude.

31. Paré, *Les idées,* 316–17.

32. Ibid., 325.

33. Ibid., 320.

34. See the articles by Payen cited in chapter 4, note 29, on the *Rose*'s possible influence on Rousseau and Diderot. Norman Cohn expresses well the view that Jean de Meun was a social thinker ahead of his time in *The World-View of a Thirteenth-Century Parisian Intellectual: Jean de Meun and the "Roman de la Rose"* (Newcastle upon Tyne: University of Durham, 1961).

35. See Payen, *La Rose et l'Utopie: Communisme Nostalgique chez Jean de Meun* (Paris: Editions Sociales, 1976), 255–58; Yvan G. Lepage, "Le *Roman de la Rose* et la tradition romanesque au moyen âge," *Etudes littéraires* 4, no. 1 (1971):91–106.

36. See the review of Fleming's *Reason and the Lover* in *Speculum* 60, no. 4 (1985):973–77.

37. See Fleming's *Roman de la Rose,* 5, for comments on Gunn's approach.

38. See, for example, François Garnier, *Le langage de l'image au Moyen Age: signification et symbolique* (Paris: Léopard d'or, 1982); Roger Pensom, "L'Allégorie de Guillaume de Lorris," *Studi francesi* 26 (1978):450–57.

39. Fleming, *Roman de la Rose,* 104.

40. Kelly, *Medieval Imagination,* 15–20.

41. For example, see Lepage, "Le *Roman de la Rose,"* 95.

42. Gunn, *Mirror of Love,* 151.

43. Ibid., chap. 2.

44. Edmond Faral, "Le *Roman de la Rose* et la pensée française au XIIIe siècle" *Revue des deux mondes,* 7th ser., 35 (September 1926):439.

45. Paré, *Idées,* 13.

46. See Paul Zumthor's analysis of the differences between the two parts based on a close analysis of linguistic factors; "De Guillaume de Lorris à Jean de Meung," *Etudes de Langue,* 609–20.

Chapter Six

1. Winthrop Wetherbee, "The Roman de la Rose and Medieval Allegory," in *European Writers: The Middle Ages and the Renaissance,* edited by W. T. H. Jackson, 2 vols. (New York: Scribner's, 1983), 1:316.

2. An excellent analysis of Jean's use of citations and *exempla* is given in Nancy Regalado's "'Des Contraires Choses': La fonction poétique de la citation et des exempla dans le *Roman de la Rose* de Jean de Meun," *Littérature* 41 (February 1981):62–81.

3. See Hill, "La Vieille's digression."

4. See Regalado, "Des contraires choses," for further discussion of the two myths.

5. Ibid., 170.

6. See Paré, *Idées,* chap. 2.

7. Regalado, "Des contraires choses," 80.

8. Ibid., 78.

9. Tuve, *Allegorical Imagery,* 259.

10. For a discussion of the paradoxical praise of an "unexpected, unworthy, or indefensible subject," see Rosalie L. Colie, *Paradoxia Epidemica: The Renaissance Tradition of Paradox* (Princeton: Princeton University Press, 1966), 3–9.

11. See Robert Hanning, *The Individual in Twelfth-Century Romance* (New Haven: Yale University Press, 1977).

Selected Bibliography

The following list includes most of the principal modern studies of the *Roman de la rose*. They have been selected for their usefulness for beginning students of the *Rose*. Specialized studies are given in the notes to the chapters. Many of the studies listed have more extensive bibliographies in which students can find other works on subjects of interest.

PRIMARY SOURCES

1. Modern editions

Langlois, Ernest, ed. *Le Roman de la rose, par Guillaume de Lorris et Jean de Meun, publié d'après les manuscrits.* 5 vols. 1914–24. Reprint. Geneva: Johnson Reprints, 1965. The standard edition for many years. Volume 1 is an introduction; the other volumes contain notes.

Lecoy, Felix, ed. *Le Roman de la rose par Guillaume de Lorris et Jean de Meun.* 3 vols. Classiques Français du Moyen Age. Paris: Champion, 1966–75. The standard edition for most scholars. Gives a summary of each section and principal variants; the extensive notes are very helpful.

2. Translations

Dahlberg, Charles, trans. *The Romance of the Rose by Guillaume de Lorris and Jean de Meun.* Princeton: Princeton University Press, 1971. Includes sixty-four illustrations. A prose translation based on the Langlois edition; more literal, less poetic than the Robbins translation (see below). Translation sometimes forced in the direction of a Robertsonian interpretation of the work.

Lanly, André, trans. *Le Roman de la rose, traduction en français moderne.* 3 vol. Paris: Champion, 1971–83. A reliable verse translation in modern French.

Marot, Clement. *Le Roman de la Rose par Guillaume de Lorris et Jean de Meung.* Edited by Silvio Baridon. 2 vols. Milan: Istituto Editoriale Cisalpino, 1954–57. A sixteenth-century edition by an outstanding poet in which the language has been modernized; includes introduction by Marot.

Ott, Karl A., ed. and trans. *Der Rosenroman.* 3 vols. Munich: Fink, 1976–79. German translation faces French text. Excellent introduction.

Robbins, Harry W., trans. *The Romance of the Rose by Guillaume de Lorris and*

Jean de Meun. New York: E. P. Dutton, 1962. Freely rendered blank verse; uses Langlois edition but does not follow lines very closely.

Sutherland, Ronald, ed. *The Romaunt of the Rose and the Roman de la Rose: A Parallel-Text Edition.* Berkeley: University of California Press, 1968. Texts printed in facing columns; introduction describes fragments and gives an excellent summary of the problems of attributing translation to Chaucer.

3. Other works by Jean de Meun

Dedeck-Hery, ed. *Li livres de philosophie.* In *Mediaeval Studies* 14 (1952):165–275.

Robert, Ulysse, ed. *L'art de chevalerie.* Paris: Société des Anciens Textes Français, 1897.

SECONDARY SOURCES

1. Studies of the *Roman de la rose*

Badel, Pierre-Yves. *Le "Roman de la Rose" au XIVe siècle: Etude de la réception de l'oeuvre.* Geneva: Droz, 1980. An exhaustive study of the influence of the *Rose* on fourteenth-century French literature. Includes good summary of the Quarrel of the *Rose.*

Batany, Jean. *Approches du "Roman de la Rose."* Paris: Bordas, 1974. A guide for students, with useful discussions of the allegorical tradition, the satire of marriage, and social questions; good bibliography.

Bourdillon, F. W. *The Early Editions of the Roman de la Rose.* London: Bibliographical Society, 1906. Still a reliable guide.

Dufournet, Jean, ed. *Etudes sur le Roman de la Rose de Guillaume de Lorris.* Geneva: Editions Slatkinie, 1984. Six articles on various aspects of Guillaume's allegory.

Fleming, John V. *The "Roman de la Rose": A Study in Allegory and Iconography.* Princeton: Princeton University Press, 1969. A thought-provoking but controversial approach to the *Rose* based on patristic exegesis.

———. *Reason and the Lover.* Princeton: Princeton University Press, 1984. Argues that the personification Reason expresses views that reflect Augustinian thinking.

Friedman, Lionel J. "'Jean de Meung,' Antifeminism, and 'Bourgeois Realism.'" *Modern Philology* 57 (1959–60):13–23. Discusses Jean de Meun's supposed misogyny in the context of traditional medieval characterization.

Gunn, Alan F. *The Mirror of Love: A Reinterpretation of the "Romance of the Rose."* Lubbock: Texas University Press, 1952. A groundbreaking study; essential for critical discussion of narrative structure and authorial intention.

Jauss, Hans-Robert. "La transformation de la forme allégorique entre 1130 et 1240: d'Alain de Lille à Guillaume de Lorris." In *L'humanisme médiéval dans les littératures romanes du XIIe au XIVe siècles.* Paris: Klincksieck, 1964, 107–46. Surveys allegorical literature in French before the *Roman de la rose.*

Jung, Marc-René. *Etudes sur le poème allégorique en France au Moyen Age.* Romanica Helvetica, vol. 82. Berne: Francke, 1971. Analyzes in detail the allegorical works preceding and contemporaneous to the first part of the *Rose.*

Langois, Ernest. *Les Manuscrits du "Roman de la Rose."* 1910. Reprint. Geneva: Slatkine, 1974. See supplementary remarks in Langlois's edition, 1:48–55.

———. *Origines et sources du "Roman de la Rose."* 1890. Reprint. Geneva: Slatkine, 1973. First detailed study of the *Rose*; still useful for a survey of sources; more information in notes to the Langlois and Lecoy editions.

Lewis, C. S. *The Allegory of Love.* London: Oxford University Press, 1936. An ambitious, stimulating discussion of major allegorical poems from the *Rose* to Spencer; includes summary of courtly literature. A landmark work and still a pleasure to read, but many of Lewis's views have been challenged by later scholars.

Luria, Maxwell. *A Reader's Guide to the "Roman de la Rose."* Hamden, Conn.: Archon Book, 1982. A useful handbook; includes discussion of many topics, such as the manuscripts of the *Rose,* Chaucer and the *Rose*; includes summary, lists of personifications and allusions, and excerpts of relevant texts. Excellent bibliography.

Muscatine, Charles. "The Emergence of Psychological Allegory in Old French Romance." *PMLA* 68 (1953):1160–82. Studies the development of the internal monologue in French romances before the *Rose.*

Paré, Gérard M. *Les idées et les lettres au XIIIe siècle: Le Roman de la Rose.* Montreal: University of Montreal, 1947. Revised version of author's *Le Roman de la Rose et la scolastique courtoise* (Paris: Institut d'Etudes Médiévales, 1941). Discusses Jean de Meun's ideas in the context of thirteenth-century Scholastic philosophy; stresses the author's Christian naturalism.

Payen, Jean-Charles. *La Rose et l'Utopie: Révolution sexuelle et communisme nostalgique chez Jean de Meung.* Paris: Editions Sociales, 1976. A study of principal themes by one of the leading French scholars of the *Rose.* Payen is the author of many articles on the work, most of which are cited in the notes to this study.

———. "A Semiological Study of Guillaume de Lorris." *Yale French Studies* 51 (1974):170–84. Analysis of the ways Guillaume uses allegorical language.

Poirion, Daniel. *Le Roman de la Rose.* Paris: Hatier, 1973. A thorough analysis of both parts of the *Rose*; perhaps the best general study of the *Rose* in French.

Tuve, Rosemond. *Allegorical Imagery: Some Mediaeval Books and their Posterity.* Princeton: Princeton University Press, 1966. Essential for medieval allegory; many perceptive ideas on the *Rose,* especially the second part.

Van Dyke, Carolynn. *The Fiction of Truth: Structures of Meaning in Narrative and Dramatic Allegory.* Ithaca, N. Y.: Cornell University Press, 1985. Good introduction to allegory; original and perceptive analysis of the *Rose.*

Wetherbee, Winthrop. "The Literal and the Allegorical: Jean de Meun and the *De Planctu Naturae.*" *Mediaeval Studies* 33 (1971):264–91.

———. *Platonism and Poetry in the Twelfth Century: The Literary Influence of the School of Chartres.* Princeton: Princeton University Press, 1972. Traces the influence of Chartrian allegory on Jean de Meun.

———. "The Roman de la Rose and Medieval Allegory." In *European Writers: The Middle Ages and the Renaissance,* Edited by W. T. H. Jackson. 2 vols. New York: Scribner's, 1983, 1:309–35. An excellent summary of the principal allegorical elements in the *Rose;* concentrates on the first part.

2. Chaucer and the *Roman de la rose*

Fansler, Dean Spruill. *Chaucer and the Roman de la Rose.* 1914. Reprint. Gloucester, Mass.: Peter Smith, 1965. Surveys linguistic evidence of possible influence of *Rose* on Chaucer.

Muscatine, Charles. *Chaucer and the French Tradition.* Berkeley: University of California Press, 1957. Analyzes the ways Chaucer's works were influenced by the courtly and realistic styles of major French works.

Wimsatt, James. "Chaucer and French Poetry." In *Geoffrey Chaucer,* edited by Derek Brewer. Writers and their Background. Athens: Ohio University Press, 1975, 109–36. An excellent introduction to Chaucer and the *Rose.*

———. *Chaucer and the French Love Poets: The Literary Background of the "Book of the Duchess."* Chapel Hill: University of North Carolina Press, 1968. Evaluates the relative importance for Chaucer of the *Rose* and the poems of Guillaume de Machaut and other late medieval French poets.

3. Historical Studies

Paul, Jacques. *Histoire intellectuelle de l'occident médiéval.* Paris: A. Colin, 1973. Discusses the *Rose* in the context of medieval philosophy.

Steenberghen, Fernand van. *La philosophie au XIIIe siècle.* Louvain: Publications Universitaires, 1966. Essential background study for the question of Jean de Meun's possible "naturalism."

Strayer, Joseph R., and Munro, Dana C., eds. *The Middle Ages, 395–1500.* 4th ed. New York: Appleton-Century-Crofts, 1959. Good general history of medieval Europe; includes chapters on the church, the universities, and literature.

Index